Miracles of Healing

INSPIRATIONAL STORIES OF AMAZING RECOVERY

Brad Steiger &
Sherry Hansen Steiger

ADAMS MEDIA
Avon, Massachusetts

Published by
Adams Media, an F+W Publications Company
57 Littlefield Street, Avon, MA 02322. U.S.A.
www.adamsmedia.com

ISBN: 1-59337-110-1

Printed in Canada.

J I H G F E D C B A

Library of Congress Cataloging-in-Publication Data
Steiger, Brad.
Miracles of healing : inspirational stories of
amazing recovery / Brad Steiger and Sherry Hansen Steiger.
p.   cm.
SBN 1-59337-110-1
1. Spiritual healing. 2. Miracles. I. Steiger, Sherry Hansen. II. Title.

BL65.M4S74 2004
202'.117--dc22
2004013269

This publication is designed to provide accurate and authoritative information with
regard to the subject matter covered. It is sold with the understanding that the pub-
lisher is not engaged in rendering legal, accounting, or other professional advice.
If legal advice or other expert assistance is required, the services of a competent professional person should be sought.
  —From a *Declaration of Principles* jointly adopted by a Committee of the American Bar
Association and a Committee of Publishers and Associations

Many of the designations used by manufacturers and sellers to distinguish their products are claimed as trademarks. Where those designations appear in this book and
Adams Media was aware of a trademark claim, the designations have been printed
with initial capital letters.

While all the events and experiences recounted in this book are true and happened to
real people, some of the names, dates, and places have been changed in order to protect
the privacy of certain individuals.

Illustration ©Charles Neal/Superstock.

This book is available at quantity discounts for bulk purchases.
For information, call 1-800-872-5627.

Foreword

AS THE AUTHORS of numerous books in Adams Media's *Miracles* series, it will come as no surprise to our readers to learn that we believe wholeheartedly in miracles—that certain physical events may occur in defiance of the laws of nature. There are many kinds of miracles, most involving some physical manifestation that is evident not only to those involved in the event, but to the people around them. When it comes to miracles involving healing, our belief is solidly based on our having been the recipients of such a blessing when we were children and our having received many subsequent healings throughout our lives.

Together and separately, we have researched the healing techniques of faith healers, Native American shamans, Indian and Asian holy men, Polynesian Kahunas, and folk healers from a wide variety of ethnic and cultural groups. We have in the course of our research observed many miraculous healings of individuals suffering from acute acne, cancer, tumors, heart problems, deafness, blindness, migraine headaches, and high fevers.

Our personal interest and extensive research in healing has taken us through unconventional or alternative modalities as well, such as shiatsu, homeopathy, visualization, radionics, chiropractic, and reflexology. We found that the ancient healing ways also have much to offer those in need of healing—meditation, fasting, color and music therapies, the laying on of hands, prayer, herbs, yoga, affirmations, mantras, acupuncture, and aroma and massage therapies. We also learned that pilgrimages or journeys to sacred places and holy shrines have brought about healing miracles for thousands of people. Healing is *healing,* and nonetheless miraculous because it came through something with which we may not be familiar.

We also have great admiration for the more conventional healing that doctors, surgeons, nurses, dentists, therapists, counselors, clergy, psychologists, psychiatrists, among many others, provide for us daily—each and every one is a miracle worker. We think it is no less a miracle if the healing comes through human hands, because they are using the divine gifts that God has given them. We consider it a great miracle that a doctor can identify and treat an illness, or that a surgeon can skillfully remove a tumor or perform heart surgery. We are thankful for all those who have devoted their lives and their special skills to share the gift of healing with others, and for all those healings that have taken place in hospitals, clinics, and emergency rooms.

This we have learned: Miracles of healing can come from many methods and modalities—some we understand, others we are only beginning to comprehend, and still others remain to be revealed. While identifying the exact *cause* of the healing is of utmost importance to scientists and healing practitioners, it is not our intention in this book to point out any one method or means over another, only to share with you some of the many accounts we have witnessed or that others have shared with us over the years.

We wish to make it clear that the *means* of healing is not definitive. God's love and power have no end. Miracles can and do happen through Divine intervention, prayer, and grace. Perhaps it is best to consider such healing as a blessed gift and mystery, not to be solved as to *how* or *why* it occurred, but to be embraced with gratitude. It is our hope that you, too, may experience a miracle and be inspired by the stories we have included in our book, *Miracles of Healing*.

*J*on Butler, a Yale University professor of American history who specializes in American religion, defined miracles as physical events that defy the laws of nature. A healing miracle occurs when an illness or a debilitating physical condition has been alleviated or cured through supernatural means, such as the power of prayer or the intervention of God or a holy figure.

A national Gallup poll released in June 2001 revealed that 54 percent of adult Americans of all faiths believed in spiritual healing and the dynamic ability of the mind, through positive thinking, to heal the body.

The May 1, 2000 issue of *Newsweek* carried the result of a survey that stated 84 percent of American adults say they believe that God performs miracles and 48 percent claim to have witnessed one. According to *Newsweek's* statistics, 71 percent of all Christians said that they had prayed for miracles regarding the healing of the terminally ill.

Stories of miracle healings are found in the scriptures of all the world religions and in churches, synagogues, temples, and mosques; contemporary Jews, Buddhists, Christians, Hindus, and Muslims still pray for and expect miraculous occurrences in their lives today.

In October 2003, Fox News released the results of a national poll conducted by Opinion Dynamics Corporation that found 82 percent of Americans of all faiths believed in miracles.

In their November 10, 2003 issue, *Newsweek* published a special issue on "God and Health" and released the findings of a new poll that revealed 84 percent of *all* Americans believe that praying for the sick improves their chances of recovery. The statistics also found that 70 percent of Americans pray often for the health of a family member.

Both the Old and New Testaments of the Bible are filled with healing miracles performed by prophets, angels, and God. The Qur'an, too, contains accounts of countless miracles, thus enabling the contemporary followers of Islam to expect such occurrences as proof of the validity of their faith.

In the New Testament, one of the principal concerns of Jesus' earthly ministry was the healing of those who sought surcease of pain and suffering. The early churches included a time for the healing of its members within the formal service—a practice that many contemporary congregations still observe as a prayer for the sick if not as an actual time for the laying on of hands.

The Roman Catholic tradition contains many healing miracles performed by saints and popes—both alive and in spirit. Father James Wiseman, associate professor of theology at Catholic University, said that there are always going to be some people "who see immediately the hand of God in every coincidence, and those who are going to be skeptical of everything. And there is a great in-between."

Rather than miracles, Philip Hefner, professor of systematic theology at the Lutheran School of Theology at Chicago, stated in an essay in *Newsweek* (May 1, 2000) that he would rather talk about blessings. "We receive blessings, often quite unexpectedly, and we want to praise God for them. We know we cannot claim the credit for these blessings. Even though we cannot predict their arrival, nor understand why so much of human life involves sorrow and evil, we can be grateful and render praise."

doctor on the staff of a large hospital in New York, who wishes only to be known as Dr. Greg, told us that he will never forget his first meeting with Bobby, a cheerful eight-year-old boy, who had been brought to the hospital with little hope of survival. Dr. Greg was an intern at the time, and he has always remembered the positive outlook of both the child and his parents, Mike and Carol. Bobby was so beautiful, so full of life, yet everyone on the staff knew that he had been carefully examined and the results of the diagnosis were conclusive: an advanced case of cancer.

When Dr. Greg spotted the head resident, Dr.

Crane, in the physicians' lounge one morning after the child had been admitted, he asked him if the results of Bobby's examination must really be considered conclusive. Perhaps there was some chance that there was some margin of error, and the family could maintain a degree of optimism.

As Dr. Crane handed Dr. Greg a set of X-rays, he told him that there was no chance of error. Bobby had an advanced case of cancer in the thighbone of his right leg. Assuming the surgical team could successfully stop the cancer from spreading, his type of cancer had a five-year survival rate at the most—and 95 percent of patients wouldn't even live that long.

Dr. Greg winced at the low odds. Dr. Crane shook his head sadly and admitted that it was neither an encouraging nor a pleasant statistic.

"Two days later, I learned something even more unpleasant," Dr. Greg recalled. "I found out that Bobby's parents had refused to allow surgery to be performed."

At his first opportunity, Dr. Greg went to the boy's room, determined to convince Mike and Carol to change their minds. He found Mike there and asked him to step out into the hall.

"I'm afraid that I was pretty full of myself in those days," Dr. Greg admitted to us. "I had ranked high scholastically in medical school, and I was proving myself under fire every day as an intern."

Although he was quite embarrassed to admit it even after all these years, Dr. Greg said that he began the conversation with Mike by asking him why he wanted to kill his own son.

Dr. Greg said that he had retained a clear mental image of the manner in which Mike narrowed his eyes and stared hard at him. "Dr. Greg, I love my son," Mike said. "I would give my life for him. Why would you say such a terrible thing to me? I am not killing him."

Dr. Greg pressed his point. "Then allow us to perform surgery. We want to save his life. We want to give him a chance to live."

Mike lowered his head, and tears coursed over his cheeks. "Dr. Greg," he began, then his voice broke and he took several deep breaths in an attempt to regain control of his emotions. "Were you on duty today?"

Dr. Greg said that he'd had the previous day off and had just returned to work.

"Yesterday," Mike continued, "Carol and I asked that more tests be run. Somehow . . . " His voice trailed off, and he stood silently for several moments, as if summoning courage to complete his thoughts. "Somehow the cancer has now spread to both of Bobby's lungs. That's why we denied surgery. Our son's time is so limited. Why subject him to any more suffering and pain than is necessary?"

Dr. Greg remembered being rocked backward as if an invisible fist had punched him in the chest. "I walked away from the poor man, feeling as though I were two inches high," he said. "How dare I come on like that to a father who was doing his best to bear his grief with a semblance of dignity? How dare I accuse such a man of wishing to kill his son? And how dare that damn insidious cancer eat away at a beautiful child's life?"

After a lengthy discussion with Dr. Crane, Mike and Carol did decide to allow Bobby to undergo radiation therapy. Shortly after the first few sessions, the game little boy suffered a very high fever.

"I had been stopping by to see Bobby from time to time," Dr. Greg told us, "and I never ceased marveling over his positive attitude and his cheerful personality. The little guy was really indomitable."

Bobby's miracle occurred as he was recovering from a second struggle with a very high fever.

"I was just entering the room when I heard him say something to the nurse and his parents," Dr. Greg said. "I will never forget the sacredness of that moment. It seemed as though one could sense something holy and loving had entered the hospital room."

The nurse asked Bobby to repeat what he had said.

"I'm going to get well now. The angels told me so," Bobby said, his confident smile lighting up his face.

"Did you have a nice dream, honey?" Carol asked her son, taking his little hand in her own. "Did you dream about angels?"

"It wasn't a dream, Mommy," Bobby insisted. "I was in heaven with angels and lots of other boys and girls. And I saw Grandpa there with his old dog, Zipper."

Mike chuckled, leaning closer to Bobby so he would be able to hear his answer. "And how are old Zipper and Grandpa?"

"Fine," Bobby smiled. "Grandpa said to tell you not to forget to give his arrowhead collection to the pioneer museum."

Dr. Greg said that he had been about to leave the boy's room, but the strange look on Mike's face caused him to stay a few moments longer. Something unusual was going on in Bobby's hospital room. He could sense it.

Later, he learned that Mike's father had died when Bobby was not quite four years old. Mike had promised his father before he died that he would transport his extensive collection of Native American artifacts to a friend's small museum in his hometown in New Hampshire, but he had never gotten around to making the trip. He could not recall ever having mentioned the unfulfilled promise to Bobby, and he knew of no way that the boy could have known of it.

"I'll get to go home pretty soon, Mom," Bobby said with an expansive smile. "The angels said that I would soon be all right. So did Grandpa."

Carol only nodded, blinking back tears.

"No one spoke at all," Dr. Greg recalled. "Who among

us wished to interrupt the little boy, who was telling us about his happy dream of angels, departed dear ones, and miracle cures when we all knew that he had only a very short time to live."

Little Bobby spoke for nearly ten minutes about having walked into a bright light and seen a beautiful angel who had taken him by the hand and led him to heaven.

"The angel told me that I was not going to heaven to stay," Bobby emphasized, "but just to rest and get all better before I came back to my hospital room. The angel said that it was not the right time for me to stay in heaven. He said that no matter what the doctors might tell me, I am going to get well!"

Incredibly, Bobby was 100 percent correct.

"In spite of about the worst odds imaginable, Bobby is now a healthy thirty-four-year-old," Dr. Greg said. "Although his condition was declared hopeless on three different occasions, he rallied each time to conquer the disease. Cancer did leave its mark on his body, however. Because the malignancy had so pervaded his right thigh-bone, his leg had to be amputated."

Dr. Greg went on to stress that none of the physicians who attended the unusual case were able to explain how Bobby's healing miracle was accomplished. "Dr. Crane wrote a lengthy paper about Bobby's case as a possible incentive to further the study of cancer by interested medical researchers. He did, however, leave out all references to angels, heaven, and spirits of the deceased."

One physician who became intrigued by the case stated that she would have to rule out the radiation therapy as having effected the cure. "The patient did have two attacks of high fever during the therapy, but this has been noted in previous cases," she said.

Another physician who served as a consultant during Bobby's time in the hospital commented that Bobby's recovery appeared to be an excellent example of spontaneous regression of cancer.

And what, exactly, is spontaneous regression?

"That's the name we doctors put on something we do not understand," admitted Dr. Greg. "In other words, a healing miracle occurred."

*T*oday, Beverly Hale Watson of Double Oak, Texas, is the highly respected author of eleven inspirational works, including such memorable titles as *Messages from the Dove, Keys to the Book of Revelation, Reflections of the Heart,* and *Death: Our Portal to Life.* In 1965, however, she was a frightened mother of two who sat in a bed in a private room on the cancer floor at Highland Park Hospital, anxiously awaiting a more complete evaluation of her medical condition. She had been told that the cysts and lumps the doctors had detected were very likely to be cancerous.

Perhaps many readers can identify with the stressful situation Beverly faced as she sat alone in her hospital room, trying her best to think only positive thoughts about the outcome of the surgery that had been scheduled for eight o'clock the next morning.

At eleven o'clock that evening, she began working on a lesson plan for the Sunday school class that she taught in order to divert her thoughts from the grim possibility that the doctors might detect cancer in her body. If the surgery provided conclusive evidence that the lumps and cysts were malignant, Beverly would be faced with the decision of how best to eradicate them.

She thought of her two small daughters and wondered if she would live to see them grow into adults with children of their own.

Mildly berating herself for considering a negative scenario, Beverly tried to focus on a more positive scene, one in which smiling doctors informed her that the cysts and lumps were benign.

As her mind tried sorting through the various courses of action that her life might take within the next few hours, she came to realize the absolute truth of the matter. She wasn't in charge of her life; God was.

Beverly remembers how precious memories started flowing through her mind in split-second intervals, followed by thoughts of things she still wanted to do. Realizing very well that she could do nothing to change her situation alone, she turned her head upward and asked that God's will be done.

"Instantly, there appeared at the foot of the bed a Light Being, whose brilliance was like the sun," Beverly recalled. "I felt tremendous love projecting toward me. At the same time, a surge of heat entered through the crown of my head, shot through my body, and exited my feet, leaving behind an inner peace that has never left me."

When the doctors operated on Beverly the next morning, they were completely surprised to find no sign of the cancer that had prompted the surgery. They were totally mystified by the change that had occurred in their patient since the last set of X-rays had been taken.

Naturally, Beverly was ecstatic to hear the good news, and it was then that she knew for certain that a miracle had taken place the night before. She decided against telling her doctors about her "visitor."

About three weeks after she was sent home from the hospital, Beverly noticed that she was beginning to predict things that were going to happen to people. She also appeared to be aware of things about certain people's pasts—and in each case, the individual was someone who had come to her for help.

For the next twelve years, from 1965 to 1977, her mentors and teachers were both visible and invisible as she concentrated on achieving higher levels of spiritual enlightenment.

Many years would pass before Beverly Hale Watson had another visit from a Light Being in completely visible form, but over the years she counted herself privileged to behold so many aspects of the "Kingdom of the Lord." As she journeyed down the path to spiritual enlightenment, Beverly remained aware of the Holy Spirit as her constant companion.

"It has presented itself in many forms," she explained. "I have heard its voice. It sounds masculine to me, and it definitely gets my attention. However, most of my information is received through thoughts, ideas, intuitions, dreams, and visions."

Beverly maintains that such spiritual information is available to everyone who can stop the constant chatter of the mind. "It is in your meditative moments that the Voice within can be heard," she said. "People go to God with an assortment of prayers, requesting assistance, answers, guidance, miracles, and so forth. They do all the talking, failing to remember that they can't hear the answers to their problems if they don't take the time to listen.

"Ask your angel guide, your Messenger of Light, to provide you with information that will be for your highest good," she continued. "A few minutes of your time spent in silence can make the greatest difference in your reality."

Beverly Hale Watson's own work as a messenger of truth continues. She considers her assignment from the Spirit to be an exciting, rewarding career that ceaselessly provides experiences beyond her wildest dreams.

"Your soul knows why you are on Earth at this point in time," she said. "The answers to all your questions can be found simply by turning within."

*L*arry told us that when he was young, it seemed as though he was always sick and missing out on school because of sinus infections, colds, hay fever, bronchitis, and every flu bug that came down the road. One night, when he was eleven, Larry nearly died, and forty-nine years later, he still believes that it was the archangel Michael who brought him back to life and cured him of a high fever and numerous allergies.

"I had suffered from alternating bouts of asthmatic bronchitis and viral pneumonia during most of the winter and early spring of my eleventh year," he told us. "I ran high fevers, and at one point I nearly starved because

Grandmom, who was looking after me, was ill at the same time; we were both too sick to realize that I wasn't taking my medicine or eating and drinking."

It was during that period of high fever and deprivation of nourishment and medication that Larry underwent a near-death experience. "All of a sudden one night, I was up near the ceiling looking down at my fevered body below on my bed," he recalled. "At first I was scared out of my wits. I thought that I had died."

Larry remembered hovering over his body for what seemed to be a very long time. "If I was dead, I began to wonder, why weren't there angels or someone to take me up to heaven? After so long of just bobbing around near the ceiling, I decided that I was not dead, but that the real me, the spirit part of me, had somehow slipped out of the body. Then I got real worried that I wouldn't be able to get back in!"

As still more time passed, Larry reconsidered his previous conclusion and decided that he really must be dead.

"Since I wasn't going to heaven, I figured that I would just be bobbing around for eternity up near my bedroom ceiling. Although I couldn't form words or make any kind of sound, I *felt* as if I were crying and calling out for help."

When help did arrive, Larry wasn't certain if he should have made a fuss. "Right next to me, there suddenly appeared the image of a big, strong man who was glowing in a kind of rainbow of blue, white, and violet colors," he told us. "In his right hand he held something that looked like a sword. When he began to speak to me, the sound of his words made me vibrate. I was never able to remember all of what he said to me, but the gist of it was that I must begin to reject the constant round of allergies and illnesses that had blighted my young life. Then he lunged at me with his sword and seemed to run me through—only it wasn't really a sword and it didn't hurt. It just kind of gave me something like an electric shock that seemed to energize me. The next thing I knew, I was back in my bed and feeling very, very hungry."

Larry remembered crawling to the kitchen and making himself some rice.

"Why I did that, I don't know. There was food on hand that didn't require cooking. I ate the rice with butter, sugar, and milk, and I started feeling better right away."

Larry told us that he continued to receive "glimpses of similar majestic beings" sporadically until he was well into adolescence, but there were no experiences as dramatic as being run through with Michael's healing sword.

According to a poll conducted by *Time* magazine in the early '90s, 69 percent of Americans believe in the existence of angels, and 46 percent are certain that they have their own guardian angels to watch over them and to guide them. Of those men and women polled by the national newsmagazine, 32 percent claim that they have personally felt the presence and/or guidance of ethereal entities in their lives.

In October 2003, a survey conducted by Opinion Dynamics Corporation for Fox News revealed that 78 percent of Americans believe in angels and their ability to interact with humans.

All religions have some kind of tradition involving an angel or spiritual guardian assigned to each individual human soul. In the ancient Sanskrit texts of the *Vedas*, the word for angel is *angira*; in Hebrew, *malakh*, meaning "messenger," or *bene elohim*, for God's children; in Arabic, *malakah*; and in India, multiwinged angels or beings are called *garudas*. As early as the third millennium B.C.E., the written records of ancient Egypt and Mesopotamia recognized a hierarchy of supernatural beings that ruled over various parts of the Earth, the universe, and the lives of human beings.

Not all angels appear as majestic beings or as powerful figures in flowing white robes. According to numerous reports from those who have experienced angelic encounters, angels have the ability to appear in a variety of forms and with a wide range of physical characteristics. They seem completely capable of shaping reality in our three-dimensional world to suit their heavenly purposes. In certain cases, they may even reveal themselves as beings of pure light.

In nearly all stories of angels, the beings appear to be both material and nonmaterial entities. Although they originate in some invisible and nonphysical dimension, they often manifest themselves as solidly in our reality as those humans whose lives they affect. There is no question that in both the Old and New Testaments, angels are considered fully capable of becoming quite physical and material—at least long enough to accomplish their appointed mission of rescue, healing, or guidance.

Although for centuries popular culture has perpetuated the idea that humans become angels when they die, the holy books of the great world religions are in agreement that angels are an earlier and separate order of creation from human beings and that humans were created a "little lower than the angels." The teachings of Islam state that there are three distinct species of intelligent beings in the universe. There are first the *malakh*, the angels that are a high order of beings created of Light; second, the *al-jinn*, ethereal, perhaps even multidimensional entities; and then human beings, fashioned out of the stuff of Earth and born into physical bodies.

Episcopal Bishop Philip Brooks once observed that there is nothing clearer or more striking in the Bible than "the calm, familiar way with which from end to end it assumes the present existence of a world of spiritual beings always close to and acting on this world of flesh and blood . . . From creation to judgment, the spiritual beings are forever present. They act as truly in the drama as the men and women who, with their unmistakable humanity, walk the sacred stage in successive scenes . . . The spiritual world, with all its multitudinous existence, is just as real as the crowded cities and the fragrant fields and the loud battlegrounds of the visible, palpable Judea, in which the writers of the sacred books were living."

ois was a child of ten when she was given a veritable death sentence. "Coldly, in front of my parents and me, the doctor said that I was very ill and was not likely to live," she said. "That night as I lay in the hospital with a half dozen or more tubes in my arms, down my throat, and up my nose, I thought that I had died when I was visited by four Light Beings. Because I was a very religious little girl, I expected to be lifted up to heaven and taken to Jesus.

"Instead of going directly to a beautiful paradise in the clouds, the angelic beings told me that the doctor had spoken the truth. I was, indeed, very ill. But although my illness could be fatal, the angels would work together and see to it that I would not die. They assured me that I had a specific mission to accomplish on Earth."

Today, as an adult of forty-seven, Lois does have two chronic illnesses, but she is still very much alive. She is a teacher of "special children" and has been active in conducting Special Olympics for the handicapped.

"Whenever I'm not feeling particularly well, I am met in my sleep by these same four angelic beings of Light, who perform some kind of vibration energy adjustments on me. Sometimes these seem to take place in an out-of-body experience," she told us. "There is no question in my mind that these angels remain emphatic about the job that I am doing with these kids. I guess both the angels and the children that I work with are an integral part of my destiny."

When Lorraine, a retired real estate agent, was eleven, she was "visited" by an angel just as she was coming down with polio in the summer of 1943.

"That was before the serum had been invented," she reminded us. "This tall, magnificent angel came to my bedside and told me that he would be with me and never leave my side. Although I became deathly ill and my parents thought for a while that they had lost me, I came through the sickness with no paralysis and no aftereffects at all."

Lorraine said that later, during her recovery, she was unable to see her protective angel, but she could hear his footsteps coming and going. "I could still 'feel' his presence even though I could no longer see him."

Her contact at age eleven initiated a relationship that Lorraine said has continued until the present day, and she is in her early seventies. "During my meditations, I consciously come into contact with an angel in a white robe, whom I recognized long ago as the same benevolent being that visited me when I was a child."

When he was eight, John, a high school teacher from Idaho, was involved in a serious automobile accident that placed him in the hospital for two months.

"My father hit an oil slick on the highway on a very rainy day," John told us. "He tried his best to control our vehicle, but we slammed into an embankment. Instantly, I was out of my body, watching other cars skid and slide to avoid hitting us. I could see my dad lying slumped against the steering wheel, but I had a sense that he would be all right."

John remembered floating through what he perceived at the time to be "a big, black, empty warehouse" until he came upon an angelic being that seemed to be composed of pure light.

"The light emanating from this entity was so bright that I remember putting up my hands to shield my eyes," he said. "After I had just floated around the being for a while, it seemed to assume a more or less human shape, and it reached out and took my hand. Everything was a blur of brilliant colors after that, and then everything went completely black."

John woke up in a body cast and in a lot of pain.

"I could just tell by the way that everyone acted that nobody thought I was going to make it," he recalled. "I could see it in their eyes. I could tell by the way the nurses never really looked at me, and it seemed like Mom and Dad were always about to cry.

"But I knew that God had sent me back for a good reason. Later, after three operations, no one, not even the doctors, could believe how quickly I healed."

John has not claimed to have had any kind of continued contact with the Light Being that took his hand and brought him back to his body, but he told us that he continued to be "a positive thinker with a lot of determination."

Dorothy, a journalist, was only thirteen when she began suffering from severe depression and a wide variety of physical disorders, including colitis, gastritis, sinusitis, anemia, insomnia, bronchitis, and circulatory problems.

"One night as I lay in my bed, I found to my horror that I simply could not breathe," Dorothy told us. "I tried to reach for my inhaler on the nightstand, but I must have blacked out. I don't really know what happened next, but I became aware of myself as a kind of orange-colored balloon floating up near the ceiling. I could look down on my body on the bed and observe it thrashing about, still trying to force air into its lungs. I really felt strangely unattached to that poor, wretched thing below, who was quite obviously dying. I actually felt relieved that my terribly afflicted physical body was dying. I felt a lot better as a balloon than as a lump of flesh beset with a dozen miseries."

While she was enjoying her newfound freedom from pain and suffering, Dorothy suddenly heard a very authoritative voice asking her an extremely important question. "I saw no one, but I distinctly heard this deep, in-charge kind of voice ask me if I wanted to live or die. I was stunned. I mean, this freedom away from my miserable body was terrific, but was I really ready to leave my parents, my friends, my school? As lousy as life could be, was I really ready to bail out at the tender age of thirteen? After all, there were things that I wanted to see and to do, regardless of my thousand and one physical torments."

The voice asked Dorothy the question again. It somehow reminded her of her stern school principal making an announcement over the loudspeaker. But what the unseen interrogator was asking was far more important than what time classes would be dismissed for Thanksgiving vacation. The authoritative voice was asking Dorothy if she wanted to dismiss her life on planet Earth for good. And she had a strong inner knowledge that whatever she decided would happen. It was really up to her whether she wished to go on living or to die.

Dorothy called out that she wished to live. "Suddenly I felt so filled with a pulsating illumination that I felt that I must be glowing like a light bulb," she recalled. "I was completely saturated with such an overwhelming vibration of love that even now, at the age of fifty-one, I cannot speak of it without crying. From that moment on, I knew that I would never be alone and that I would be able to handle any suffering, pain, or adversity that might come along in my life."

And then Dorothy was back on her bed, still gasping for her next breath, trying desperately to force air into her lungs.

"It truly was as if time on the physical plane had stood still," she said. "I finally managed to grab my inhaler and blast a cloud of its life-sustaining medicated mist into my lungs. Within the next few minutes, I had once again regulated my breathing."

That next week, Dorothy was diagnosed with hypoglycemia, and she at last found her way to a nutritionist-endocrinologist who helped her on the path to restored health.

On December 12, 2000, the London *Times* reported on the two-year study of the phenomenon of guardian angels that was conducted by Emma Heathcote, Birmingham University researcher. Heathcote's study, the first academic research into the subject of angels, examined the stories of more than 800 Britons who claimed encounters with heavenly beings. Almost a third of those who contacted the researcher reported seeing a traditional angel with white gown and wings. Another 21 percent saw their guardian angel in human form. Others experienced the sensation of a force around them or being engulfed in light.

One of the more dramatic accounts in Heathcote's research was the instance in which an angel appeared during a baptism at a village church in Hertfordshire in front of thirty witnesses, including the rector, church-warden, and organist. Confirming the story for journalist Carol Midgley, the rector said that he was baptizing a twenty-two-year-old woman who was about to be married but had never been christened. Suddenly there appeared before the baptismal "a man, but he was totally different from the rest of us. He was wearing something long, like a robe, but it was so white it was almost transparent." The angelic figure didn't have wings, and he simply stood there silently, looking at those assembled for the baptismal service. Children came forward with their mouths open. People said later that they felt as if "warm oil" had been poured over them. Then, in a few seconds, the angel was gone. But, the rector stated, the appearance of the angel had changed the lives of everyone present that day.

Other witnesses of angelic activity told Heathcote stories of seeing guardian angels at hospital beds and deathbeds, ministering to the ill or manifesting to escort souls to heaven. A good number of accounts reported the appearance of majestic beings to allay people's fears, to let them know that they were not alone in dangerous or stressful situations.

Rather than external entities presenting themselves to provide assurance of a celestial helping hand, psycho-therapist Dr. Susan Blackmore theorizes that angel sightings are merely apparitions created by the brain in times of crisis in order to provide comfort. Though she might agree with Dr. Blackmore that certain angel sightings might be "crisis apparitions," Ms. Heathcote returns to the baptism in the church in Hertfordshire as an incident to give the staunchest critic pause to wonder: "I interviewed a lot of people about that angel," she said, "and everybody told the same story. Their descriptions were totally consistent."

Emma Heathcote said that although humans have been preoccupied with angels for centuries, we may now be going through an increased period of interest in the heavenly beings because "people are feeling a spiritual shortage and angels fill the gap." In her opinion, men and women in contemporary times fashion their own faiths in what often seems like a "spiritual supermarket" of choices available to them. "They might take a bit of Christianity, a bit of Judaism and Buddhism, together with a belief in angels to create their own eclectic religion," she said.

In June 1992, while she was traveling with her father, Mike, and her sister, Gillian, eight-year-old Gemma Quinn from Woolton, Merseyside, UK, received severe spinal injuries in an automobile accident. Gillian had a broken back, from which she recovered, but Gemma was paralyzed from the neck down and was told that she would not be able to move anything below her shoulders. She would never walk again. It would be her lot in life to be always reliant on a ventilator and a wheelchair.

Gemma never gave up hope that she would be able to walk again. She knew that there must be some way for her to get back on her feet. Those who knew Gemma were impressed with her resolve and her determination, and in 1996, she received a Child of Courage award.

In February 2003, Gemma was taken to London to begin a form of mind therapy known as Mind Instructor. Her initial success with the technique, which involves intensive mental exercises, along with some physical therapy, encouraged Gemma to move to London. She felt that she had discovered the kind of mental and physical processes that would enable her to walk once again, and she wished to concentrate on the methods taught at the Mind Instructor Clinic by her therapist, Hratch Ogali.

In October 2003, eleven years after the automobile accident, nineteen-year-old Gemma took her first steps. She said later that she was really quite surprised. Initially, she took just a couple of steps. The next day, she managed six, then twenty.

When speaking with journalists about the miracle healing, Gemma acknowledged that she still had a lot of work ahead of her, but those beginning steps had felt wonderful—and so natural. She was now more confident than ever that she would walk again. In fact, for her father's recent birthday, she had made a video of her cycling, kicking a ball, and walking.

Her instructor, Hratch Ogli, described Gemma Quinn as an amazing woman who had triumphed over the negative predictions that she would never walk again.

While John Cavenagh of the Spinal Research Charity stated that it was very good that Gemma was able to stand up and begin to walk after eleven years of paralysis, he told the BBC on October 8, 2003 that one really couldn't term the Mind Instructor techniques as therapy for spinal injuries in general. "What [the mental exercises] are probably doing is unlocking some residual function that she has, that she hasn't been able to make use of before," he said.

*T*he unlocking of some mysterious, miraculous, mental healing potential within each human being is known to many individuals as the power of positive thinking, and many serious researchers believe that this remarkable energy can be controlled by the human will.

In the last years of the nineteenth century, French medical doctors and psychologists became enthusiastic about experiments in healing through hypnotism. For a time, these pioneers in psychosomatic medicine believed that patients needed only to be hypnotized in order to be restored to a state of vibrant health by the power of suggestion. One of the most important schools of curing through suggestibility was established in 1882 by a distinguished French pharmacist named Émile Coué, who became known as the master of the mind cure.

Coué came to believe that the key to the healing powers of the mind was to be found in repeating mental suggestions when the mind is most receptive to messages. This, he maintained, occurred immediately after a person is awakening from a deep sleep or just prior to falling asleep.

Every morning and evening, Coué's advice was to repeat the words: "Every day, and in every way, I am getting better and better." He told people not to think about the meaning of those words. They were devised to telegraph the message of positive mental and physical health to the subconscious mind.

Émile Coué had stumbled onto what he believed to be a very interesting psychological truism. When the *will* and *imagination* are battling, he stated, imagination will always win. If the sufferer's mind is filled with doubt and fear, it becomes difficult for any doctor to cure any disease.

Coué said that the phrase "I can" is the release. In his opinion, it is our imagination, not our willpower that transmits an idea into the subconscious mind. Once an idea has been placed in the subconscious, anything is possible because it is the subconscious mind that rules the physical body. Imagination, Coué insisted, can be trained more rapidly than willpower. And, brilliant pharmacist that he was, Coué firmly stated that from a medical point of view, this technique was not intended to replace more conventional therapeutic approaches, but to accompany them and perhaps to enhance them.

According to Coué's ardent followers, his healing suggestions were able to cure virtually every type of illness, and his "I can" incantations swept the world. Schools were established, and books were printed on the art of suggestibility.

Later, after becoming a fad in the United States in the 1920s, Couéism was shown to have limitations. Perhaps some people were unable to believe and self-doubt would cloud their minds. Scientists were unconvinced of the power of suggestibility to actually heal patients. Nevertheless, the repetitive "Every day, and in every way, I am getting better and better" did produce some remarkable cures for many people, and Couéism gave birth to many so-called New Age mental healing techniques.

Émile Coué died in 1926, but his books continue to be reprinted, and his influence continues to spread the concept of healing through autosuggestion throughout the world today. Among well-known, modern-day exponents of Coué's theories are Rev. Norman Vincent Peale, Rev. Robert Schuller, Dr. Carl Simonton, and Dr. Bernie Siegel.

*P*hineas Parkhurst Quimby (1802–1866) is known as the gentle father of mental healing. It became his mission to help everyone to understand how they could use the mind to influence the body and alleviate suffering and disease. Although he began his adult life as a clock maker and an inventor, he had always nurtured a deep interest in people. Quimby did not possess an extensive formal education, but he read voraciously, especially material on philosophy and science.

Quimby made no sudden conversion from clock maker to mental healer, but rather came to his conclusions slowly; his opinions evolved over periods of time after much deliberation. Quimby came to the conclusion that medicine had little effect on a patient. It was, he decided, the patient's faith in the cure that did the healing. Quimby began investigating this notion until he decided that suggestion alone was powerful enough to cure.

Quimby's method consisted of developing great empathy for and kinship with the patient while allowing the patient to gain complete confidence in him. In some cases, Quimby would place his hands upon a patient; he claimed that this only focused the patient's attention on the healing and was most effective when the patient believed that such touches would heal him. In fact, Quimby took no credit for the healing at all. He maintained that he acted like a lens that focused the healing power of the patient's mind onto his or her illness or pain.

Quimby lived a simple life. His neighbors admired and respected him, and he had a reputation in the community as an honest, gentle, and practical man. He regarded his healing work as a method of correcting the errors that humans themselves had made. Since God is good, and so is His creation, Quimby reasoned that humans must have come to experience sickness as a result of their own mistakes. Thus, he declared, humans could correct these errors with their mind.

Quimby's most famous patient was Mrs. Patterson of Bow, New Hampshire, who is known to the world as Mary Baker Eddy, the founder of Christian Science. In

1862, she came to Quimby after years of suffering from cataleptic fits and unexplainable pain. His alleviation of her maladies had a profound effect on her founding of the Christian Science movement.

Quimby hoped that the woman, who professed to be an authoress, might use her talent with the pen to pass on what she had learned with such patient endeavor. She returned to him in 1864 and studied with him, using his manuscript entitled *Questions and Answers*. After Quimby's death on January 16, 1866, Mary Baker Eddy praised him in print, giving him full credit for his influence on her thought. Quimby's pioneering work laid the foundation of many schools of thought, including Christian Science, New Thought, and Metaphysical Healing.

*K*ent, a successful architect from Oregon, told us that he received a miracle healing of his bleeding ulcers in a very special dream.

"I was reared in a Protestant tradition," he said, "but I have never really been what anyone would deem a religious person. But in this extremely vivid and detailed dream, I saw myself in biblical times in a courtyard setting. I was dressed in a blue and white robe, sitting on a bench before a wooden table that was loaded with all kinds of food and pitchers of wine. There were men and women dressed in colorful, elegant robes seated around me, laughing, eating, and drinking."

And then, Kent went on to warn us, came the part of the dream that some people found to be inspirational, and others found a bit far out. Kent saw a handsome, distinguished, bearded young man approaching him, who he intuitively knew was a representation of Jesus as he might have appeared at the time of his teaching and healing ministry in ancient Nazareth. Jesus wore a white robe with a kind of red shawl across his shoulders. He smiled at Kent's table partners and indicated that he wished to sit next to Kent. The couple nearest Kent obliged Jesus by sliding over to make room for him at Kent's right side.

"My Brother," Jesus said in a voice of quiet authority, "I am happy to see you here among us at this festive occasion, but I am saddened to learn that you have suffered great pain in your stomach."

Kent was astonished that he knew of his physical complaints, but then he reasoned, he is, after all, Jesus. He undoubtedly knew everything about Kent.

Kent explained to Jesus that the doctors said that he had a very bad case of bleeding ulcers that had become so advanced that the condition would soon require surgery.

"You worry too much about too many things that are really beyond your control and are really not that important," Jesus said. "Ever since you were a small boy, you have fretted about the most inconsequential matters. It is one thing to be conscientious about the performance of one's responsibilities; it is quite another to be obsessed with the trivial aspects of your work. You must learn to let go and to let God. You must trust in your Heavenly Father to run the universe. If He cares about the number of feathers on a sparrow's wing, you must believe that He cares about you."

Kent agreed in essence with the words of Jesus, but he wondered how he could cease instantaneously to be the compulsive worrier that he had always been. He also realized that the surgery would do him little good if he did not learn to control the nervous energy that had caused a series of upset stomachs, a spastic colon, and now the resultant bleeding ulcers.

As if Jesus had read Kent's thoughts, he answered, "Nervous energy will become productive expression when you learn to trust the Father to be quite capable of running the universe without your believing that you have to assume a prominent role in managing planet Earth."

The men and women at the table laughed and nodded their heads approvingly. The man opposite Kent reached across the generous banquet feast and squeezed his hand, as if to offer encouragement. Kent felt awkward when it occurred to him that the entire company at the table had been listening to the conversation that he had been having with Jesus.

"But first, before we repair your faith," Jesus said as he reached for a bowl of what appeared to be assorted slices of various kinds of fruits, "let us heal your stomach."

Kent involuntarily shrank back as Jesus handed him what looked like a slice of citrus fruit.

"I'm sorry," Kent apologized. "My doctor told me to avoid any kind of citrus fruits. Too much acid, you see."

The woman seated at Kent's left made a clucking sound with her tongue as if to scold him. *"Your doctor?* Dear Brother, you are in the company of the Master Physician, the great healer. Take the fruit that he offers you. You should be thankful that he has taken notice of your ills."

The heads of everyone at the table were nodding their agreement. Reluctantly, Kent accepted the slice of fruit and gingerly placed it in his mouth. He was amazed at the texture, and at the sensation that it prompted from his taste buds. The fruit was somewhat pulpy, a bit tangy, but it made his mouth feel cool. It had kind of an apricot taste and feel, but there was also a touch of some kind of berry.

"Although this all took place in a dream," Kent told us, "I could somehow feel the soothing coolness of the mysterious fruit in my throat when I swallowed it."

Jesus smiled, and Kent said that his dinner companions in the dream applauded his compliance. Kent remarked that he felt like a small boy being encouraged to eat all of his vegetables.

"And eat some of these nuts," Jesus told Kent as a man brought another bowl to the table. "They have been coated with special herbs. Take a generous handful and eat them with great relish."

Once again, Kent protested that his doctor had warned him against ingesting such harsh roughage as nuts and popcorn.

And once again, the looks of astonishment from his fellow guests, appalled that Kent would dare question the Great Healer, forced him to place a handful of the nuts into his mouth without another word of objection.

"I know it was a dream," Kent assured us once again, "but I actually felt my teeth grinding and crunching the nuts and the herbs. And the taste was so unusual, like nothing that I have placed in my mouth before or since. A hint of black walnut, perhaps a light dash of cashew, but the herbs transformed the nuts into a wondrous element far beyond the standard repertoire of my plebeian taste buds."

When Jesus handed Kent a cup of wine, he now knew better than to argue that his doctor had warned him that alcohol would really upset his ulcers.

"Believe me," Kent remembered Jesus told him, "this wine is like no other that you have ever tasted. There is pure love and light distilled into the fruit of the vine that offers the strength of earth and sun."

Kent said that he nodded as if he completely understood the words of Jesus, and he emptied the cup without removing its rim from his lips.

"As the wine filled my stomach," Kent said, "I experienced a healing of my internal wounds. The touch of the wine was soothing and cool, and my entire body seemed to glow with its curative power."

"Trust in the Father," Jesus told Kent. "And be calm and at peace."

Kent awakened with those words of Jesus echoing in his mind. It was 4:15 A.M.

His wife told him that he had been tossing and turning in his sleep; she thoughtfully inquired if his ulcers were troubling him and asked if she should bring him his medicine.

Kent told her that he felt certain that his ulcers had been healed by Jesus in a dream and that he believed that he would never need his medicine again. She mumbled, "That's nice, dear," and fell back asleep.

"But that morning at breakfast, when I told her the dream in its entirety, she prayed with me that Jesus' healing of my ulcers would come true," Kent said. "Two days later, at my regular appointment, my doctor confirmed that my condition was so greatly improved that surgery would no longer be necessary if I continued to get better. Although he was clearly astonished by my sudden and dramatic improvement, he gave me a bunch of new prescriptions and encouraged me to 'keep doing whatever I was doing.'"

Kent never got the prescriptions filled, and three weeks later, after an extensive examination, his doctor enthusiastically agreed that the bleeding ulcers had improved to such an extent that no additional medication would need to be prescribed.

It was at that point that Kent told him about his dream of Jesus healing his ulcers, and the doctor was diplomatic enough to say that there were many things that medical science could not explain.

"My wife and I will always believe that the Divine Physician did heal me in that vivid dream experience," Kent told us. "I have slowly learned to stop worrying about the little things in life, and my new attitude of tranquility has prevented any recurrence of the ulcers."

om Whitehead of Festus, Missouri, told us that there have been two occasions when his life has been saved by prayer. The first miraculous healing occurred when he was six years old, in 1956, and living with his parents in the little town of Bernie, Missouri.

Tom told us the story of his first miracle in these words:

"I have had asthma since I was a few weeks old. Back then, medicine was not as advanced as it is today. I can remember lying in a dark room with the door open a crack and hearing Doc Kelly telling my mom and dad that I probably would not live till morning. I remember Dad coming into the darkened room and sitting in a chair beside the bed. I remember him holding my hand and starting to pray. At some point, I fell asleep. This is one of my earliest memories. I survived that night, even though the doctor had given up and left. I believe it was Dad's prayers that brought me through."

The second time that Tom believes his life was saved by prayer was in March 1989.

"Dad had been killed in a fall at work many years before," Tom told us. "We were now living in Festus, Missouri. I had been very sick for nearly two weeks. Since the flu was going around at the time, I thought I just had a bad case of the bug. My stomach felt sore, and I could barely get off the bed. My skin had turned gray, and I finally realized that whatever I had, it was not the flu."

Tom made an appointment with their family doctor and drove to his office in Crystal City the next day.

"Once in the examination room, the nurse stuck a thermometer in my mouth and took my pulse," Tom recalled. "When she took the thermometer out and looked at it, she gave me a strange look and hurried out of the room."

A short time later the nurse returned with the doctor right behind her. He informed Tom that he was very sick and had to go to the hospital immediately.

Tom explained that he had borrowed his brother Joe's car. He first had to take the car home so Joe could go to work. Joe could drop him off at the hospital on the way to his job.

"The doctor said I had to go to the hospital at once, and he told the nurse to call an ambulance," Tom said. "I don't remember how it was decided, but the nurse drove me the two blocks to Jefferson Memorial Hospital in her Volkswagen "Bug" rather than wait for the ambulance. I was taken up to the fifth floor surgical unit since my doctor, Dr. B.A., was chief of surgery and head of J.M.H. emergency medicine. I was packed in ice to try to lower my temperature, which was 108 degrees. My mother, Bernice Whitehead, and my Aunt June were allowed a brief visit."

Sometime during the late night hours, Dr. B.A. came into Tom's room and said that Tom had to tell him the truth. Tom was surprised by the surgeon's demand for truthfulness, since he had no reason whatsoever to be less than honest with him.

"He asked me if I had ever had any rare diseases," Tom recalled. "He quizzed me about any rare tropical disease that I might have picked up. I told him I had not had any rare or unusual illness, and I tried to remember every sneeze and cough I had ever had since childhood."

Completely puzzled by the doctor's strange interrogation, Tom was even more baffled when the surgeon shouted at him, "Then there's nothing I can do. I don't know what to do!"

Next, Tom remembered, Dr. B.A. stomped out into the hall and started yelling at nurses. "He had the whole floor in an uproar," Tom said. "Nurses were scurrying in all directions; even an orderly was upset. I heard them yelling to each other, 'Don't touch the patient without gloves.'"

Tom knew that the staff was talking about him.

"After a while some nurses and an orderly came into my room with a red box that had the word 'Contaminated' stenciled in white letters," Tom said. "They had something like a broom handle with which they picked up my clothes and put them in a trash bag. Then they dropped everything into the box. The orderly said that they were moving me to intensive care and that they had to call someone in my family."

Tom recalled that he didn't want them calling his mom the way they were carrying on. He was afraid they would frighten her. "I told them to call my brother, Joe," Tom said. "For some reason, I thought that since he had been in Vietnam, he would be able to handle this kind of thing."

By the time Joe arrived at the hospital, Tom admits that he was an emotional wreck. "I've had it. It's all over for me," he said to his brother.

"Joe told me I had to calm down, and he would go get the preacher," Tom said. "Joe looked as scared as I did. The preacher and Mom arrived soon after. By the time they left, I was calm and ready to accept whatever God had in store for me."

Time became something of a blur for Tom over the next several days. "I was poked, jabbed, stuck, radiated, and turned every which way but loose," he told us. "The only thing the medical staff seemed to know for certain was that I had peritonitis and gram negative septicemia. Finally, Mom and my sister, Terrie Jones, were told that I had no more than twelve hours to live."

After receiving such a grim death decree from the doctors at Jefferson Memorial Hospital, Tom said that he could only remember bits and pieces of the next few hours. "I seemed to fade in and out," he said. "I was cold all the time. Incessantly, I shook violently from the fever. I remember the nurse coming into the room and putting some electrodes on my chest. She asked me to help her, but I was too weak. I was then wheeled to pre-op."

Later, Tom learned that his mother and sister had convinced the surgeon to do an emergency exploratory surgical procedure. Although the surgeon agreed to perform the procedure, he went on record as saying that he didn't believe Tom had an operable problem and that he would probably not survive the surgery.

"In pre-op, I could only see things as if through a white cloud," Tom remembered. "I don't know if that was due to the low light level in I.C.U. and then the bright lights of the pre-op or not. I remembered seeing [someone] whom I assumed was the anesthesiologist, as a black silhouette. I remember thinking how much that dark form looked like my dad. He was 5' 11" and stocky build, and was bald except for the sides. Then I must have had an audio hallucination because I heard a woman's voice ask me something. I told her I was cold. I was sure she said: 'You have to go through three rooms, each colder than the next.' This was nonsense, because the operating room was through the double doors no more than ten feet away. I just accepted what she said without question."

The next thing Tom remembered was being on the operating table. He could see Dr. B.A. and another surgeon, Dr. V., who was assisting in the operation. "When they noticed me trying to hear what they were saying," Tom said, "they went out and stood by the door to talk. I felt so sick that I wanted this to be over. I knew I would not survive, but I just wanted it to end. I was ready to die."

Tom said a final prayer, which he remembers was, "Lord, I have gone as far as I can go. It's in Your hands now."

He looked around the room and saw the anesthesiologist looking at him with what appeared to be pity. Tom saw him make some motions, and he felt the anesthetic hit him. For some reason, Tom tried to fight the anesthetic, but his eyes closed against his will.

Since the afternoon that Tom had been rushed to the hospital from the doctor's office in the nurse's Volkswagen and his mom had learned that his condition was serious, she notified her church and placed her son on a prayer list. Relatives were called in southeast Missouri to place Tom on their prayer lists.

"Although I had many people praying for me, I will always remember Marla Derm and her husband," Tom told us. "Marla preaches at a church, and she has been a friend of the family for many years. She told her husband that they had to pray for a healing, and they went into a private room to kneel and pray. I remember her saying that they prayed for hours. At first she said she could see a black cloud hanging over me. But as they prayed, the cloud left. She said she knew then that their prayers had been answered and that I would make it. She also said that she saw something milky white on my stomach.

"Well, of course, I did make it through the operation," Tom said, concluding his dramatic story of a miracle healing. "I had a polyp that had burst. They said it may have happened a year or more before I got sick. Poisons had been leaking into my system for a long time."

What about the "milky white object" that Marla had seen on Tom's stomach? "After the operation, I was left with a temporary colostomy to give the bowel a rest," Tom explained. "The surgeons had to cut six inches off my intestine and my liver was 'shot full of holes.' Those colostomy bags can only be described as milky white. They were worn just to the left and a little below my navel line."

In Tom Whitehead's opinion, he survived the serious illness and the emergency surgical procedure that the doctors predicted would be fatal, all because of a healing miracle prompted by the power of prayer.

*A*ccording to a survey taken by Lutheran Brotherhood reported in *USA Today* (February 7, 1997), Americans are great practitioners of prayer: 24 percent of those polled said that they prayed more than once a day; 31 percent prayed every day; 16 percent, several times a week; 10 percent, several times a month; and 9 percent, several times a year.

A 1999 CBS News poll found that 80 percent of adult Americans believe prayer improves recovery from disease.

In June 2001, a national Gallup poll revealed that 54 percent of adult Americans believed in spiritual healing.

The results of a *Time*/CNN poll (*Time*, June 24, 1996) stated that 82 percent of those surveyed believed in the personal power of prayer to heal; 73 percent believed that their prayers could heal others of their illness; 77 percent expressed their faith that God could sometimes intervene to heal people with a serious illness; and 65 percent indicated that a doctor should join their patients in prayer if so asked.

Prayer (*salat*) is one of the five Pillars of Islam, and the true believer must say his prayers (*salla*) five times a day, as well as on special occasions. The set schedule of prayers—dawn, noon, afternoon, sunset, and nighttime— are strictly prescribed and regulated. There is another category of prayer, the *du'a*, which permits spontaneous expressions of supplication, petition, and intercession. The *du'a* may also be allowed after the uttering of the formal *salat*.

Jewish liturgy did not begin to achieve its fixed form until the centuries after the destruction of the second temple, and the prayer book did not appear in its classical form until the Middle Ages. But spontaneous prayers are found throughout the *Tanakh*, the Hebrew Bible, and the Old Testament in the Christian Bible. There is a rich Jewish tradition that envisions angels carrying human prayers to heaven, and there is a belief that the entreaties of the righteous can more effectively intercede with God than ordinary mortals.

In recent years, more and more doctors and scientists have begun to study the power that many religious men and women claim may be achieved by focusing their prayers upon God and asking healing for themselves or others. In June 2000, researchers at Duke University Medical Center in Durham, North Carolina, presented the results of a six-year study in the *Journal of Gerontology* in which nearly 4,000 mostly Christian men and women sixty-five and older were asked about health problems and whether they prayed, meditated, or read the Bible. Dr. Harold Koenig, one of the researchers, stated that this was one of the first studies showing that people who pray live longer. Relatively healthy seniors who said that they rarely or never prayed ran about a 50 percent greater risk of dying during the six-year study compared with those who prayed at least once a month. People who prayed even once a month appeared to get the same protection as those who prayed more often.

Dr. Larry Dossey, author of *Healing Words: The Power of Prayer and the Practice of Medicine*, recalled when he was doing his residency at Parkland Memorial Hospital in Dallas, Texas, and had his first patient with a terminal case of cancer. Whenever he would stop by the man's hospital room, Dr. Dossey found him surrounded by visitors from his church, praying and singing. Dr. Dossey thought this was appropriate since they would soon be singing and praying at the man's funeral, because the cancer had spread throughout both lungs. A year later, when he was working elsewhere, Dr. Dossey learned from a colleague that the terminally ill patient was alive and well. When he had an opportunity to examine the man's X-rays, Dr. Dossey was stunned to see that his lungs were completely clear. There was no trace of cancer. Although Dr. Dossey had long since given up the faith of his childhood, it seemed to him that prayer had healed this man of his terminal cancer.

Intrigued, but devoted to the power of modern medicine, Dr. Dossey became chief of staff at a large urban hospital. He observed that many of his patients prayed, but he put little trust in the practice. It wasn't until he came across a study done in 1983 by Dr. Randolph Byrd, a cardiologist at San Francisco General Hospital, in which half of a group of cardiac patients were prayed for and half were not. Those who were prayed for improved in a significant number of ways. Dr. Dossey could no longer ignore the evidence. The Byrd study had been designed according to rigid criteria. It had been a randomized, double-blind experiment—neither the patients, nurses, nor doctors knew which group the patients were in.

Inspired to search for other such experiments, Dr. Dossey was astonished to find more than 100 serious and well-conducted studies exhibiting the criteria of good science. About half of these studies demonstrated that prayer could bring about significant changes in those suffering from a variety of illnesses. Dr. Dossey has since given up the practice of medicine to devote himself full-time to writing about and researching prayer and how it affects human health. His extensive studies have produced such discoveries as the following:

1. The power of prayer does not diminish with distance. It can be as effective from the other side of the world as it is from the next room.
2. There is no right way to pray. There is no difference in the effectiveness of the various religious methods of praying.
3. Rather than asking for a specific healing for a particular health problem, the nonspecific prayer, "Thy will be done," works as well as or better than attempting to specify the outcome.
4. Love added to prayer increases its power.
5. Prayer is outside of time. It can be answered even before it is made.
6. Prayer is a reminder that we are never alone.

Gordon, the well-dressed gentleman in his mid-fifties who invited us to join him for dinner one night after our seminar in Los Angeles, seemed to be the very image of propriety. It was difficult not to appear somewhat shocked when he made a startling confession: "At the age of twenty-one, I was more animal than human," he said. "I had been drinking for a mere five years, yet I was a completely warped personality. When I was seventeen, my alcoholism drove my family to have me removed from the home for the sake of the younger children."

Gordon told us that he had joined one of the armed services, hoping that military discipline would help him reconstruct his life. But violence had become his constant companion. Berserk escapades, blackouts, straitjackets, hospitals, jails, and detention barracks became his principal environmental scene. Officially, during that brief period of time, he was charged and convicted a total of thirty-eight times for military and civilian infractions of the law.

By the age of twenty, Gordon was a social misfit who had abused every agency that had offered him assistance. Everyone who knew him regarded him as an unstable troublemaker.

Somewhere on his angry path to self-destruction, Gordon had attended a meeting of Alcoholics Anonymous.

"I could see it was a good program," he said with a smile, "for alcoholics, that is. But, of course, I didn't consider myself in that category. Somewhere in their literature, though, I read the words, 'God as I understand Him' and 'a Power greater than myself.' It simply didn't occur to me at the time that these two simple expressions offered the very spiritual and physical emancipation that I had so longingly pursued."

After that brief flirtation with A.A., Gordon yielded to the seductive siren call of the bottle and entered into a month-long binge.

"When I finally sobered up enough to recognize my own face in the bathroom mirror, I was horrified by my ghastly reflection," he said. "I had the shakes, and the entire room seemed to be pitching like a small boat on a stormy sea."

Gordon walked to a bridge over a river and strongly considered suicide.

"Instead, thankfully, I called a man whom I had met during one of my few visits to an A.A. meeting," he told us. "He came to my foul-smelling room and told me his own story of human degradation that almost made my fall from grace seem insignificant. He had deserted his wife and three children. He had broken into homes and stolen objects to pawn. He had even robbed elderly men and helpless women and children on the streets—all to support his miserable partnership with John Barleycorn. The love of God had at last enabled him to put his wretched, wicked ways behind him and to enter the twelve-step program of A.A.

Gordon was greatly moved by the man's unmistakable depth of sincerity, and after his new friend had left, he sat up late into the night, reading verses from the Bible and passages from *The A.A. Way of Life* until he fell asleep.

He found himself fascinated by the revelation experience described by "Bill," the cofounder of Alcoholics Anonymous, as he lay in a hospital: "My depression deepened unbearably," Bill confessed, "and finally it seemed as though I were at the very bottom of the pit . . . I found myself crying out, 'If there is a God, let Him show Himself! I am ready to do anything, anything!'

Suddenly the room lit up with a great white light. It seemed to me . . . that I was on a mountain and that a wind not of air but of spirit was blowing. And then it burst upon me that I was a free man. Slowly the ecstasy subsided. I lay on the bed, but now for a time I was in another world, a new world of consciousness. All about me and through me there was a wonderful feeling of Presence . . . "

Gordon hadn't prayed since he was a boy, but that night he prayed for hours with great power and conviction that he would be filled by the Holy Spirit and be given the strength to exorcise alcohol from his life forever.

Sometime during the night, Gordon experienced the first in a series of dramatic spiritual encounters. He told us that when he recounted his experience for others, as he was doing for us that evening, it was as if he could still feel the almost electric vibrations that seemed to fill his body and every corner of that dark, dismal room.

"I saw an illuminated vision of Jacob's ladder," he said. "At the base of the ladder, I witnessed a fierce death struggle between a dark-clad person and one clothed in white garments. It was a fight to the death—and I knew that both of the combatants were aspects of myself. Praise God, the white-clad warrior was victorious, and the vision disappeared.

"I awakened shaking with joy and great excitement. I knew that freedom and a new life were now mine.

I have not taken a drink since—and that was over thirty years ago.

"Think of it," Gordon emphasized as he concluded his moving account. "Years of slavery to the sickness of alcoholism were vanquished in one night after I prayed and asked God for the strength to burst free of my dependence on the bottle."

ince Dr. Herbert Benson's seminal research at Harvard University in 1972 demonstrating the influence that the mind can have over the body, 92 out of 125 medical schools offer courses in nontraditional healing methods. In his *The Relaxation Response*, Dr. Benson showed how patients could successfully battle a number of stress-related illnesses by practicing a simple form of meditation. Dr. Benson, president of the Mind/Body Medical Institute of Boston's Deaconess Hospital and Harvard Medical School, has suggested that 60 to 90 percent of all visits to doctors are in the mind-body, stress-related area, and the traditional medical ways of treating such patients through prescription medicines or surgeries are not effective in such chronic cases. Perhaps, more and more researchers are discovering, faith can make a sick person well.

Dr. Jeffrey Levin of Eastern Virginia and Dr. David Larson, a research psychiatrist with the National Institute for Healthcare Research, have located more than 200 studies that touch directly on the role that faith and religion may have in the healing process. Among such interesting research studies were a 1995 study performed at Dartmouth-Hitchcock Medical Center, which found that heart surgery patients who drew comfort and strength from religious faith were more than three times more likely to survive; a thirty-year study on blood pressure, which showed that churchgoers have lower blood pressure than nonchurchgoers, even when adjusted for smoking and other risk factors; a 1996 National Institute on Aging study of 4,000 elderly, which found that those who attend religious services are less depressed and physically healthier than those who don't attend or those who worship at home; and numerous studies in which non-churchgoers have been found to have a suicide rate four times higher than regular churchgoers and much higher rates of depression and anxiety-related illnesses.

In *Timeless Healing*, Dr. Herbert Benson states that those patients who claim to feel the intimate presence of a higher power have generally better health as well as increased chances for much more rapid recoveries. He writes that the human genetic blueprint has made a belief in an Infinite Absolute a part of our nature in order to offset our uniquely human tendency to ponder our own deaths: "To counter this fundamental angst, humans are also wired for God."

*T*hirteen-year-old Nicola Pacini, who lived with his family near Florence, Italy, had been confined to a wheelchair for five years with muscular dystrophy when his parents decided to take him to visit the Virgin Mary shrine in Medjugorje in December 1991.

In spite of the popularity of Medjugorje as a healing shrine, Nicola did not want to go; he told his parents that he would rather have them save the money that such a trip would cost. Nicola thought that it would be useless to go and that the pilgrimage would only bring all three of them additional heartache and disappointment.

Nicola argued that he was but one of millions of

handicapped people in the world, and he would be but one of thousands of pilgrims who would be crowding around the statue of Mother Mary at Medjugorje praying for a healing. Why would the Queen of Heaven choose him before all the others?

But at last, after much discussion and prayer, Nicola agreed to accompany his parents to the holy place where Mother Mary had appeared wearing a crown of twelve stars.

The bus trip was exhausting, but when the Pacini family arrived at the shrine on December 8, Nicola's mother wasted no time in pushing his wheelchair directly in front of Mary's life-size statue. Perhaps more to please his parents than to get a miracle, Nicola began to pray.

Then, to his astonishment and his parents' great joy, he felt his paralyzed right hand slowly open.

Encouraged by such a marvelous sign of divine energy, Nicola was eager to return to the shrine the next morning. In his prayers, however, he asked that his healing not be done for his sake alone, but also for that of his parents'.

And then, Nicola simply felt like getting up and walking—for the first time in five years.

It was the strangest feeling, Nicola said later. It was as if something were moving inside of him, and he had an overwhelming urge to get up and walk. An irresistible force seemed to be lifting him up from the wheelchair.

Although he thought that it was impossible, he found himself standing upright and walking!

After he had taken the first few steps, he called out to his mother and heard her cry of joy, as a miracle had occurred. Mrs. Pacini instinctively rushed to her son's side to help him, but Nicola asked her to leave him alone. He knew that he could walk on his own.

The Pacini family will always remember how the hundreds of pilgrims who were gathered around the shrine burst into applause when Nicola kept walking.

The boy's mind was filled with the wonder of it all. Mother Mary had heard his prayers and those of his parents.

When the Pacinis returned to Florence, Dr. Rosella Mengonzi, their physician, was shocked when she saw Nicola standing and walking. Dr. Mengonzi had been certain that Nicola would be forced to spend his life in a wheelchair. After a thorough examination, Dr. Mengonzi told journalist Silvio Piersanti that somehow Nicola Pacini had completely recovered from an incurable disease in a manner that she could not medically explain. A healing miracle had been performed.

any people of faith find that a pilgrimage to a holy shrine or icon can accomplish miracles of healing. Among the most famous in the world is the healing Grotto of Massabielle, popularly known as the Grotto of Bernadette at Lourdes, France, which was constructed on the spot where Bernadette Soubirous had the vision of the Virgin Mary in 1858. Since the time the miracle occurred for the young miller's daughter, pilgrims have journeyed to Lourdes to seek healing from the waters of the natural spring that appeared in the hillside after the apparition of the Virgin Mary appeared before Bernadette. Consistently, for decades, an average of

200,000 people visited the shrine every year. During the centennial celebration of Lourdes in 1958, more than two million people came to the tiny community in southern France to seek a healing. In recent years, average annual attendance has risen to over five million. In 2001, there were six million pilgrims who sought a miracle from the waters of Lourdes.

Hundreds of thousands of cures have been claimed by men and women who immersed themselves in the cold spring waters of the shrine. In addition to the physical blessings bestowed upon certain pilgrims, there are also healings of a spiritual nature, such as faith and conversion, and of a psychological nature, such as freedom from anxiety and compulsion. Only the cures that are allegedly of a dramatic physical nature are investigated by the Lourdes Medical Bureau, and of the many thousands claimed, only sixty-six have been officially proclaimed as miracles. The bureau, established in 1883, has insisted that the following criteria must be met before they will certify a cure as an example of a miraculous faith healing:

1. The affliction must be a serious disease. If it is not classified as incurable, it must be diagnosed as extremely difficult to cure.
2. There must be no improvement in the patient's condition prior to the visit to the Lourdes shrine.

3. Medication that may have been used must have been judged ineffective.
4. The cure must be totally complete.
5. The cure must be unquestionably definitive and free of all doubt.

Over ninety years ago, Dr. Alexis Carrel, who won the 1912 Nobel Prize in physiology and medicine, stated that he had observed with his own eyes a vicious cancer sore suddenly transform into a scar. This miracle, he said, occurred after devout prayer and a pilgrimage to Lourdes by Marie Bailly, a patient of Carrel's colleague and well-known Bordeaux surgeon, Dr. Bromillous.

Dr. Bromillous told Dr. Carrel that the patient's entire immediate family had died of tuberculosis. Marie Bailly had tubercular sores, lesions in her lungs, and she had been afflicted with peritonitis for several months. The poor woman could have died at any moment, but several of her relatives had demanded that she make the trip to the healing shrine at Lourdes.

Dr. Carrel examined Marie Bailly's thin white face and was dismayed by its emaciated condition. The young woman's abdomen was twisted into a misshapen lump. Her ears and nails were already turning a vivid blue. Her pulse beat raced at an incredible 150 beats a minute.

Dr. Bromillous asked Dr. Carrel's opinion after they had left the patient.

Dr. Carrel shook his head sadly. "She's doomed."

Such a pronouncement by Dr. Alexis Carrel would have been considered definitive by any group of physicians. Until his death in 1944, he was one of the foremost medical authorities in the world. An American surgeon and an experimental biologist, Carrel won the Nobel Prize in 1912 for his extensive work in suturing blood vessels and transplanting organs. Working with Charles A. Lindbergh, he invented the mechanical heart. He also developed a method of keeping human tissue and organs alive in nutrient solutions.

There was no question that Dr. Carrel was an eminent medical authority and that his diagnosis of a patient's condition would likely be accurate. However, when he pronounced Marie Bailly doomed, he had not taken into account the miraculous healing powers of faith.

As Dr. Carrel and his French colleagues drove to Lourdes to observe the activities at the shrine, the

American doctor made no secret of the fact that his religious ideals had been destroyed by his scientific investigations. In the nature of intellectual curiosity, he had, on previous occasions, accompanied groups of patients to Lourdes, but he professed to be a skeptic among the devout pilgrims. As a scientist, he was only interested in examining the claims of alleged cures, but he personally gave little or no credence to them.

Dr. Carrel admitted that everyone had been very kind in opening medical records for his examination, but in his considered opinion, too many of the alleged cures could be the result of a form of hysteria rather than an organic disease. The only thing that would convince him of a healing miracle, he stated, was the cure of an organic disease, such as a cancer disappearing, a bone regrowing, or some congenital dislocation completely vanishing.

Certain French doctors argued that they had presented the skeptical Carrel with documented records of such cures as those that he had mentioned, but the American surgeon protested that none of those cures had occurred in front of his own eyes, and he did not examine the patients before and after the alleged healing. Dr. Carrel made it clear that he was not demeaning the analyses of other doctors, but he proclaimed that he personally could not accept the reality of such alleged miracle healings. If he should witness such fantastic phenomena for himself, Dr. Carrel stated, he would toss away all of the scientific theories and hypotheses in the world. And he would do so gladly, for such miracles would reaffirm his belief in a higher power.

By the time that Dr. Carrel and his colleagues arrived at the healing shrine at Lourdes, there were hundreds of pilgrims gathered around the spring. Glancing about the crowd, he saw Marie Bailly standing in front of the shrine. Her weariness betrayed her, and the feeble movements she made were those of a dying creature. Although he was well accustomed to illness and death in all of their unpleasant manifestations, the sight of the suffering woman clutched his body like an iron fist.

Suddenly Marie Bailly stiffened as if she had been struck by a powerful force that now surged through her pain-wracked body. The stretcher-bearers nearby stared incomprehensibly at her, and one of them fell to his knees and crossed himself.

Dr. Carrel and his colleagues watched with astonishment as Marie's face clouded momentarily, and her paleness was replaced by a rosy hue.

Before the doctors' eyes, her swollen abdomen was transformed from a misshapen lump into a flattened, smooth stomach. Her pulse calmed, and her respiration appeared to be normal.

"I would like a glass of milk, please," Marie asked feebly.

As she eagerly swallowed the milk, the doctors noted that it was the first food or drink that she had been able to consume in almost a week.

Since Dr. Carrel had witnessed the amazing healing, he did not trust his ability to remain objective without other doctors as witnesses during the re-examination. When he returned to the Sept Douleurs hospital, the shaken scientist requested that three other physicians assist in the examination.

Later, one of the French doctors shrugged and told Dr. Carrel that they could only verify what he already knew—that Marie Bailly had been cured.

Dr. Carrel tried to reconstruct the miracle that he had just witnessed and make it fit somehow with the reality that he understood. Only an hour before, the young woman had been dying. He knew this to be a fact, for he himself had examined her thoroughly before she had been taken to the healing waters of Lourdes. She had suffered for years from tuberculosis—an organic disease. Her cure had fulfilled all the criteria that he had insisted must be present to satisfy his cynicism regarding supernatural acts of healing.

After receiving the miracle cure, Marie Bailly recovered quickly and returned to her home as a completely well person. The dank stench of death no longer hung over her. She seemed literally to be reborn after her long illness, and her body appeared to glow with health and vitality.

Just as Marie Bailly was cured of her terminal illness at Lourdes, so did Dr. Alexis Carrel leave his skepticism to be submerged in its healing waters. He was transformed from a rigid scoffer into a devout believer in the power of faith to accomplish miraculous healing.

The Lourdes Medical Bureau, established in 1883, has noted more than 2,500 cases of healing that they considered truly remarkable, but that fell short of their strict criteria of a miracle. Since 1958, the Church has acknowledged only six miracles occurring at Lourdes. The most recent healing to be so accredited occurred to mill worker "Jean-Pierre Bély" from western France, who had been stricken with multiple sclerosis in 1977. The disease left him almost completely paralyzed, unable to walk, and nearly as helpless as an infant. He had to have someone help him shave, get dressed, and perform daily hygienic tasks.

Bély was taken to Lourdes in 1987, and one morning before he was taken to the shrine, he prayed to the Blessed Mother to grant him a healing. Then, to his complete astonishment, in the next moment she appeared to him and told him to get up and walk.

As he later described the apparition to others, Mother Mary had blue eyes and was smiling at him. She was very young and beautiful, dressed all in white, but was barefoot. She commanded him to stand, but Bély confessed that he was so in awe of the presence of the Blessed Mother that he was petrified with fright.

Later, after his son had helped him bathe in the waters before the shrine, Bély was deeply disappointed when nothing happened to alleviate his condition. He remained paralyzed, unable to stand. Perhaps, he reasoned, he had offended Mother Mary by not obeying her command to stand when she appeared before him.

The next day, however, when he was resting in his hospital bed, he suddenly felt an icy chill move through his body. Then, in the very next moment, a fiery heat came over him. At first the sensation of heat was mild, then it became difficult for Jean-Pierre to endure.

It was then that he comprehended that he had been healed. He swung his legs over the side of the bed and stood up without assistance. He stretched both his arms and his legs to be certain that he had been cured—and took his first steps in years.

As he moved forward, feeling very much like a child learning to walk, he began to weep for joy, crying and hugging his wife. With tears streaming down both of their faces, Jean-Pierre and his wife thanked God and the Blessed Mother for his miracle.

A representative from the Lourdes International Medical Bureau agreed that there was no scientific explanation for Jean-Pierre Bély's recovery and decreed it to be a true miracle. Some of the most accredited multiple sclerosis specialists in Europe agreed that Bély's healing was much more than a remission—which, they acknowledged, could possibly occur over several months. Bély's recovery, however, had occurred literally overnight, which was inexplicable.

After sixteen years of almost complete paralysis, Jean-Pierre was able to walk with his wife, carry groceries home from the market, ride his bicycle, and visit the sick to inspire them with hope for their conditions.

The priest who had organized Bély's pilgrimage to Lourdes expressed his opinion that there was no medical explanation for such a miraculous cure. In 1999, the Church officially recognized the healing of Jean-Pierre Bély as the first true miracle at Lourdes in a decade.

For quite some time, Mrs. Josephine Hoare had suffered from chronic nephritis, a severe kidney disease. In 1972, however, when her doctors gave her only two years to live, she decided that a trip to Lourdes would give her a greater chance to enjoy the future.

When the twenty-eight-year-old housewife from London returned home, she claimed that she had been blessed with a healing miracle from Mother Mary. To silence any doubters, she returned to her physicians to verify the miracle that she was certain had occurred.

While they admitted that the disease had become inexplicably dormant, they were reluctant to acknowledge a full-blown Lourdes miracle. Although Josephine joyfully declared that she was about to begin a new life—and a family—her doctors sternly warned her never to attempt to have a child. According to their scientific and medical expertise, pregnancy could very well activate the disease and would almost certainly kill her.

Josephine, however, believed in the miracle that Mother Mary had awarded her, and she soon became pregnant. Once again, Josephine Hoare claimed divine intercession. Her doctors admitted that they were completely confounded, and on December 30, 1973, they announced that mother and child were doing well. While Josephine Hoare's miraculous healing may not be officially recognized by the Church, the divine blessing that she received was good enough for her.

✛

The Roman Catholic Church is well aware that most miracles are born in the hearts of believers and require no blessing or approval from an ecclesiastical hierarchy.

Father Frederick Jelly, professor of systematic theology at Mount Saint Mary's Seminary in Emmitsburg, Maryland, has served on miracles committees and has listed the questions asked to authenticate a miracle as the following:

- What is the psychological state of the person claiming the miracle?

- Is there a profit motive behind the miracle claim?
- What is the character of the person who is claiming the miracle?
- Does the miracle contain any elements contrary to scripture or faith?
- What are the spiritual fruits of the miracle—does it attract people to prayer or to acts of greater charity?

Once these questions have been determined and reviewed, the committee makes its decision as to whether or not the event was heavenly inspired. If the committee decides the event is miraculous and its implications have national or international effect, the case may be referred to the Vatican's Sacred Congregation for the Doctrine of the Faith in Rome. The Sacred Congregation has the authority to institute a new investigation and make its own ruling and recommendation to the pope, who is the final arbiter of miracles.

In the late 1870s, the village of Knock in County Mayo, Ireland, was in the midst of a terrible famine. In desperation, fifteen devout villagers gathered in the little Catholic church to ask for deliverance from the unrelenting pangs of hunger that had weakened them all.

As they prayed for divine help, they were amazed to see a glowing light beginning to form at one end of the small church. As the astonished villagers gazed, spellbound, at the brilliant light, they were able to distinguish the figures of Mother Mary, St. Joseph, and St. John standing at the altar, looking upward at a lamb surrounded by golden stars.

Ten days after the villagers had experienced the vision, a young girl born deaf was instantly given the gift of hearing. Within a few weeks, many ill, diseased, or crippled people who visited the church began to claim miraculous cures as they knelt at the statue of Mary.

In 1879, clerical authorities from the Roman Catholic Church were sent to Knock to investigate the alleged vision and the numerous cures ascribed to the holy visitation. After the clerics had spent several days interrogating the villagers who had witnessed the apparition and the people who had received miracle healings, they stated their official conclusion that an authentic manifestation of the Blessed Mother had occurred.

At the close of 1880, more than 300 cures, all deemed miraculous, were recorded in the diary of the parish priest. Since that time, the small village of Knock has come to be called the "Irish Lourdes," and medical authorities continue to be astounded by the number of healings that have taken place at the little church's shrine.

✛

When he was just a boy of ten in the 1960s, Nicholas Doyle of Bray County was stricken with rheumatic fever. Doctors said that the boy's heart had been so severely affected that, in addition to being forbidden to participate in even the mildest forms of exercise, Nicholas had to be confined to his bed. He was denied even the gentle exertion of knitting as a means to pass the time.

In desperation, Nicholas's parents decided to bring him to the holy site in Knock to beseech a miracle. Just a few days after he had been blessed before the statue of the Blessed Mother in the village church in Knock, Nicholas was riding his bicycle. The Doyles' family doctor found himself completely at a loss to explain the miraculous cure.

✚

Bridie Hopkins, a teenager from Leeds, England, suffered from a diseased leg bone. She testified that after she had received the blessing at the shrine in Knock, the numbness in her leg disappeared and there came a strange kind of prickling sensation.

Four months later, doctors pronounced Bridie's leg completely healed.

In 1994, Dr. Patrick O'Mara stated that Marion Carroll's miraculous recovery from multiple sclerosis defied the laws of science and medicine as he had previously understood them.

Although Mrs. Carroll, a resident of Athlone, Ireland, began having symptoms of multiple sclerosis in 1972, the disease wasn't diagnosed in the young mother until 1978. By then, she had lost the use of both of her legs.

Her husband, Jimmy, got her an electric wheelchair, but her hands soon became too weak to work the control button. Then, the muscles in her throat were stricken, and she couldn't speak or swallow properly.

She had to drink with a straw, and she was unable to hold her head up without a neck brace. When it seemed that her physical condition could not be worse, Marion developed epilepsy and kidney infections. Her husband and her two children took turns washing, changing, and feeding her.

Then, on September 3, 1989, forty-one-year-old Marion agreed to allow some friends to take her by ambulance to the statue of Mary at Knock. After all, what did she have to lose? She had heard the priest say that he was already choosing the kind words that he would say at her funeral.

Marion Carroll was carried into the church on a stretcher and placed under the statue. Later, she told journalist Fleur Brennan that she didn't have the will to pray and beseech the Blessed Mother for a healing. She simply said to Mary that she, too, had been a mother. She would know how Marion felt about leaving her husband and children.

A few minutes later, during a religious service in the village church, Marion felt a strange sensation moving over her. She knew that some unseen force was urging her to walk.

She didn't want to make a spectacle of herself before the statue of the Blessed Mother, so she waited until she had been carried out of the church before she convinced her nurse to undo the straps on her stretcher.

Immediately, Marion was propelled to her feet by that same unseen force. She felt herself completely filled with love, and she rose from the stretcher and began to cry tears of joy.

When Marion Carroll returned home and showed her husband and children that she could walk, there were many more tears of joy and thanksgiving. Jimmy told her that he had been earnestly praying that she would receive a cure.

Dr. Patrick O'Mara, the Carrolls' regular physician, together with a physical therapist, conducted a thorough examination of Marion and declared that the muscles, which had been shriveled for eleven years, were now totally normal. In addition, the epilepsy and kidney problems that had so afflicted her had also disappeared.

Although patients suffering from multiple sclerosis do have remissions, they generally take place over a period of time. Dr. O'Mara told Fleur Brennan in November 1994 that Marion Carroll's case was different because she had regained her full health instantly. Dr. O'Mara reinforced his earlier diagnosis and treatment, and stated that Marion Carroll's multiple sclerosis had been as bad as any that he had ever seen, and she did not have long to live. He simply could not explain what happened. It appeared that Our Lady of Knock had worked another miracle.

In 1979, on the centennial of the apparition, Pope John Paul II visited Knock. While he was there, he, together with the crowds that had gathered to welcome him, experienced a visitation from Mary in which the Holy Mother blessed the village of Knock.

*I*n spite of current popular interest in such matters as spiritual healing, many medical doctors remain highly skeptical of any claims of miraculous cures through such unconventional methods as prayer and pilgrimages. The American Medical Association, however, has long recognized the power of faith on the individual mind as a factor that may affect the condition of those who are ill, and they do not quarrel over the fact that such "miracles" do occur.

In an official statement released many years ago, the A.M.A. freely admitted:

"There are occasional instances in which diseases generally regarded as uniformly fatal reverse themselves without any explainable medical cause . . . But the medical profession does not recognize that 'faith healing' as such has any accepted merit whereby it can be regarded as having remedial or curative effect in persons who are actually victims of organic disease."

Despite detractors, serious interest in the topic of spiritual healings has surged in the past thirty years—whether the cures have resulted from the laying on of hands, the power of prayer, or faith in a divine being.

Dr. Larry Dossey, former chief of staff at Medical City Dallas Hospital and author of *Healing Words: The Power of Prayer and the Practice of Medicine,* has declared that the potentiality of prayer to heal need no longer be regarded as just a matter of faith. In his book, Dr. Dossey cites more than 130 studies, most of them conducted in the past thirty years, which encompass a wide variety of religions and different prayer styles.

"I have come to regard [prayer] as one of the best-kept secrets in medical science," Dr. Dossey has remarked. "When people enter a prayerful state of mind, good things happen to those they pray for."

Writing in *A Doctor Heals by Faith,* British physician Christopher Woodward affirms his belief that "the next great step forward . . . is the realization of the existence of healing powers on the spiritual level which, as yet, have not been understood—though they were seen very clearly when Christ was on earth."

Dr. Paul Tillich was on the staff of Harvard University's Divinity School when he wrote The *New Healing* in 1955 and expressed his disapproval of the long neglect of Christ-centered spiritual healing by the world's Christian clergy.

"The gospels, certainly, are not responsible for this disappearance of the power in the picture of Jesus," the respected theologian observed. "They abound in stories of healing; but we are responsible ministers, laymen, theologians, who forget that 'Saviour' means 'healer,' he who makes whole and sane what is broken and insane, in body and mind."

An Episcopalian minister who conducts regular healing services told us that it was his belief that "when the spirit, body, and mind are unbalanced, illness follows. With God's help, we can pray and restore the proper balance."

A surgeon who practiced at a major metropolitan hospital admitted his personal philosophy that modern medicine must always be conducted with compassion and hope.

"I often pray throughout the entire time that I am performing surgery," he said. "If a complete healing does not occur, I still consider the prayer answered if the patient is given the strength to be able to live with his or her illness."

✚

The contemporary mystic Harold Sherman was firm in stating that one should never pray out of a sense of duty, obligation, or habit. One should not make a ritual of getting a prayer over with as quickly as possible. Nothing is accomplished by rapidly mumbling a prayer without thought or feeling behind it. It is the feeling behind a prayer, Sherman advised, not the words thought or spoken, which gets through to God-level of mind.

In his book, *How to Solve Mysteries of Your Mind and Soul*, Sherman presented "Seven Secrets for Successful Prayer":

1. Remove all fears and doubts from your mind before you start to pray.
2. Make your mind receptive so it is prepared to receive guidance and inspiration.
3. Picture clearly in your mind what it is that you desire to bring to pass in your life.
4. Have unfaltering faith that with God's help what you are picturing will come true.
5. Repeat your visualization and your prayer . . . until what you have pictured becomes a reality.
6. Review each day's activities and constantly strive to improve your mental attitude, so your mind can become a clearer channel attuned to the God Power within.

7. Realize that if your thinking is right and if you persist with faith and put forth every effort in support of your prayer, then that which you create in your mind must eventually come to pass.

In the early 1930s, a cargo-laden freighter was trapped in a battering storm off the coast of Cromer, England. Exposed to the icy waves and gale-like winds, two sailors roped themselves to the ship's mast to prevent being washed overboard.

Several hours later, after the storm had moved out across the sea, the unfortunate sailors were brought to shore by rescue crews, who worried about the blue tinge on the men's faces. As the rescuers wrapped the unconscious sailors in warm blankets, they feared that the men were near death.

Moments later, Dr. Edward Bach arrived at the rescue scene. He pressed a small vial of fragrant liquid to the lips of an unconscious sailor. The sailor stirred visibly, his ice-encrusted eyelids flickering. A few minutes later, both men were sitting up and sipping hot tea, apparently none the worse for their ordeal.

An astonished seaman who had volunteered for the rescue party was shocked by the sailors' sudden recovery and wondered what the doctor had in his bottle.

Dr. Bach explained that he had given the nearly frozen men a healthy dose of his rescue remedy, a mixture of the essence of five flowers brewed into a single liquid: cherry plum, clematis, impatiens, rock rose, and the star of Bethlehem. He had put the sailors on the road to full recovery with his flower power.

By 1934, Dr. Edward Bach developed an unusual form of healing remedies, and "flower power" testimonials filtered into his office from throughout the world. A graduate of the University College Hospital, London, and later a house surgeon there, Dr. Bach gradually became more interested in his patients than in their illnesses. After many years of sitting at the bedsides of men and women afflicted with various maladies, Dr. Bach decided that the real cause of many illnesses was the worries that they suffered.

In 1913, Dr. Bach assumed a post at University College Hospital as the casualty medical officer. During World War I, he was in charge of a 400-bed hospital for war injuries, and it was at this time that he began to observe the effects of stress and trauma upon the recovery of his patients.

After working in the National Temperance Hospital and later establishing a successful private practice, Dr. Bach began investigating the healing power of flowers that had been developed by Dr. Samuel Hahnemann, the father of Homeopathy. Both Paracelsus and Hippocrates had suggested earlier the possibility that flowers contained healing liquids.

Dr. Bach used a very simple process to obtain the essence of the thirty-eight flowers that he prescribed. He collected the blossoms of flowers on a warm, sunny day. He placed the blooms in a large glass bowl containing pure spring water. The bowl was then left in warm sunlight for at least four hours.

The blossoms were then carefully picked out of the bowl, leaving the water with the essence of the blooms, the living extract of the flowers. The water was poured into bottles and prescriptions were then filled from the stock bottles. Drops of the concentrated solutions were diluted with more pure spring water and usually taken with milk or water.

In spite of publishing his clinical results in several medical journals, the Bach Method became controversial among medical men throughout the world. Dr. Bach believed patients were capable of diagnosing their own illness. "Treat the patient, not the illness," was a favorite statement of the flower-power healer.

In Dr. Bach's opinion, intelligent persons should be capable of making their own diagnosis. Doctors should take no notice of the disease. Instead, they should analyze the outlook on life of the patient in distress.

Dr. Bach believed every disease to be the outgrowth of some failing in the patient. He maintained that fear, worry, anxiety, and depression are the causes of disease. A physician should seek out the true cause of a patient's illness. Heal the cause and the disease will disappear, Dr. Bach argued.

Dr. Bach maintained that the only equipment needed for a diagnostician was complete and total honesty. He outlined thirty-eight basic mental moods, which created disease. These criteria were further classified into seven distinct categories that included Uncertainty, Loneliness, Despondency, Fear, Oversensitivity, Apathy, and Overcare for the Welfare of Others.

Dr. Bach set forth five principles to consider when diagnosing disease.

1. The soul of man is our real selves.
2. Life is our school of experience.
3. Our time on earth is but a moment in the total evolution of the soul.
4. When the soul and the personality are in harmony, the individual will experience happiness, vibrant health, and peace.

5. Unity is the key of all life and the creator of unity is love.

Dr. Bach told his patients that two serious errors of the mind that inevitably led to disease were cruelty to others and a failure to honor the dictates of the soul. He believed that disease was the result of conflict between the soul and the mind and could never be cured except through spiritual and mental effort.

Although Dr. Bach was a practicing physician, a noted medical officer, and a registered bacteriologist, there has always been considerable opposition to his flower remedies. The British Medical Association declared his remedies to be nothing but a bunch of perfumed placebos. If a person should have a heart attack, conventional doctors asked, would he or she want the services of a coronary specialist or a vial of flower juice?

Edward Bach died on November 27, 1936, but the Dr. Edward Bach Centre in the UK carries on his work. The Bach Centre contains thousands of testimonials to the effectiveness of flower remedies, and there are many sworn affidavits from seriously injured persons who were saved by Dr. Bach's famous Rescue Remedy. Dr. Bach's book, *Heal Thyself: An Explanation of the Real Cause and Cure of Disease*, remains in print.

Although the medical profession as a whole continues to reject the essence of flowers in their practices, today there are hundreds of physicians, chiropractors, osteopaths, and other healers who prescribe flower remedies for their patients. Only time will enable us to determine the exact worth of Dr. Edward Bach's unusual claims of healing.

The year is 1940. The narrow-chested, weak-chinned man on the padded table receiving a massage from a master masseur is Reichfuhrer SS Heinrich Himmler, second officer of the German Reich. As we focus on the scene, the high-ranking Nazi official is engaged in a familiar argument with his masseur. In a half-joking, half-serious tone, the officer snarls that he must break the man of his one outrageous flaw—his love of Jews.

The masseur smiles, but allows none of his true feelings to show in his facial features. Instead, he kneads the Nazi officer's back more gently. "Perhaps it is because I see them as part of the human race," he replies in a soft voice.

The officer growls that the masseur should listen more closely to the Führer, the mesmerizing Adolf Hitler.

As the Reichführer's temper rises, he reminds the masseur that he could have him shot, tortured, dismembered, or sent to a concentration camp.

The masseur acknowledges that his patient has such power, but he knows Himmler will not carry out such a threat; Himmler knows this as well. The Reichführer has become completely dependent upon his masterful massages to ease his awful stomach pains.

"You must calm yourself," he tells the officer. "You must relax and allow my fingers to work their magic."

"Ach," Himmler snorts in disgust. "How many must we release this time?"

"I have a list for you to sign," the masseur says evenly, the lips on his smooth face barely moving as he speaks.

For a moment, sparks seem to fly from the Nazi's eyes, then he relaxes and the massage continues. A few moments later, the high-ranking officer emits a long sigh of gratitude, his terrible stomach pains once again relieved by the ministrations of the skillful masseur.

"Give me the list," he says gruffly. "I will sign it. Felix Kersten, you are the most abominable necessity I've ever had."

To that, the masseur smiled confidently.

+

Before the Nazi power structure was broken by the Allies at the conclusion of World War II, Kersten managed to bargain his skillful massages for the lives of thousands of Jews and political prisoners who would have perished in the Nazi death camps.

Felix Kersten, a Finnish citizen who was born in Estonia in 1898, had studied agriculture until he joined the army of Finland during World War I. Although the art of massage had become very sophisticated in Finland, Kersten had no inclination to study it until after the war, while he convalesced from a wound in a Helsinki hospital.

Contemplating the future, the opportunities seemed very limited. Although he had been trained in agriculture, Kersten no longer had any land to work, and his army career had ended abruptly with his wound. Besides, he did not desire to follow the military arts.

Every day, he interacted with men he admired—the doctors who cared for him. Kersten resolved to join their ranks, but when he confided in a doctor about his newfound ambition, the man discouraged him. The doctor patiently explained the years of necessary schooling, which would not be easy for a man with no preliminary training or funds. The doctor then suggested that the young Kersten begin a study of massage.

"Your hands are ideally suited for it," the doctor explained, looking at Kersten's short, powerful fingers.

After a little more conversation, the doctor had convinced the young officer to at least talk to the masseurs on the hospital staff before dismissing the notion of massage altogether. With his first attempts, Kersten found that he had a gift for the art, and the hospital staff was astounded at his great talent. He became the favorite masseur for all the soldiers who came to the Helsinki hospital. Kersten experienced great joy when he discovered that he could bring health and comfort to men's wounded bodies with his hands.

The young masseur came under the tutelage of a well-known specialist named Dr. Killandar, and Kersten soon became his devoted pupil. Although he never missed a lecture, class, or demonstration, Kersten worked part-time to earn enough money to eat while he studied. By 1921, he received a degree in scientific massage, and Dr. Killandar told his prize pupil that he would have to journey to Germany to further his studies.

Once again, the masseur paid his rent by working at odd jobs in Berlin. Although never able to live an affluent life, Kersten kept his good spirits through patient devotion to his work.

He studied under a famous surgeon and teacher, Professor Bier. Though accepted as a medical authority in every corner of the world, this well-known physician had idiosyncrasies, which often disturbed his more conventional colleagues. He had a practice of investigating the alternative methods of healing, and his open-minded devotion to the single goal of alleviating suffering often brought him criticism in the drawing rooms of Berlin.

Through Bier, Kersten met a Tibetan monk named Dr. Ko. The small, elderly man had come from Asia to complete his study of the masseur's art. Kersten first accepted the monk only because Bier had introduced them, but he later found that the old man, whose face wore a perpetual smile, knew approaches and techniques no Western masseur had ever thought of attempting. Where Kersten had thought himself quite accomplished in the art of massage, Dr. Ko quickly convinced him that he knew very little.

Backed by centuries of study and tradition, Dr. Ko introduced Kersten to Asian massage. The Finn had not studied the monk's techniques for very long before he realized just how primitive Western methods were. Asian massage incorporated facets of Yoga and metaphysical philosophy in which the masseur built a bond of great empathy between himself and his patient.

Most important to the treatment of pain was the diagnosis of cause, and most important to the diagnosis were the sensitive fingertips of the masseur. To be a successful masseur, the pupil had to devote his entire being to the art, and this Kersten did with great zeal, ignoring his poverty and meager diet to concentrate on the teaching of Dr. Ko with a frenzy that approached obsession. He admired the monk, not only as a skilled practitioner of massage, but also as a man. Dr. Ko had great fortitude, courage, and endurance, and he cheerfully accepted all that life offered with the smile that forever graced his face.

For a time, Kersten seemed set adrift after the monk bade him goodbye and returned to his Tibetan monastery. Word, however, of Kersten's great talent as a masseur spread throughout Europe. Perhaps his most famous pre–World War II patient was the Prince Consort, husband of Queen Wilhelmina of the Netherlands. The man suffered from severe stomach pains, which only Kersten could relieve.

During the war, Kersten found himself a virtual prisoner of Heinrich Himmler, who suffered from the same stomach disorder as the Prince Consort. Only Kersten's nerve therapy gave Himmler any relief from his severe abdominal pains, and the Reichführer became completely dependent on the masseur's soothing fingers.

Kersten's expertise and his absorption of Dr. Ko's wisdom led him to pronounce Himmler's severe stomach convulsions as the result of much more than the effects of overwork and stress on a weak physical constitution. In his opinion, the Nazi leader suffered from the conflict engendered by a psychic division, which had begun early in life. Kersten realized that Himmler could never really be cured, because the basic cause of the stomach pains was within the man's psyche.

In 1940, the Gestapo moved Kersten and his family to Berlin so that he might attend to Himmler at the Reichführer's slightest whim and need. It was here that Kersten used his position to great advantage. Together with certain trusted friends, he would make a list of the people he wanted exempt from the concentration camps. The lists would be several pages long with plenty of space at the bottom of each page. When Himmler signed off on the list after Kersten had ceased the officer's fierce abdominal pains, the masseur would add many more names.

After a year of providing surcease of stomach agonies for Himmler, Kersten managed to establish a secret network of communications with intelligence agencies in England, Sweden, and Finland, utilizing the Nazis' own telephones. It was extremely advantageous to the Allies to have a contact who could operate within the Nazi headquarters in Berlin.

In 1941, the masseur convinced Himmler to disobey Hitler's command to resettle 8.5 million Dutch and Flemish citizens. As the Reichführer told Kersten of the Führer's orders, the masseur told his patient of the terrible toll that such a massive undertaking would have on his condition of intestinal cramps and colic. Perhaps, he worried Himmler, even his special nerve therapy would not be able to help him if he were to collapse under the strain of such an exhaustive enterprise.

In 1945, Kersten arranged a meeting between Himmler and Norbert Masur, a member of the Swedish branch of the World Jewish Congress. Due to Kersten's incessant badgering, Himmler agreed to refuse Hitler's order to kill the 60,000 Jews who remained in the concentration camps before their liberation by the Allies.

After the war, Kersten received official exoneration from a charge of collaborating with the Nazis. The Netherlands made him a Grand Officer of the Orange-Nassau for his personal intervention, which saved many Dutch lives and much Dutch treasure from the Nazis. Charles de Gaulle bestowed the Legion of Honor on Kersten for his efforts in saving the lives of French Jews and other French citizens whom the Nazis had marked for execution. By the time of his death in 1960, Felix Kersten, the healer with the magic touch, had been nominated for a Nobel Peace Prize nine times.

*I*n November 1994, Lee, a Manchester (England) Metro-politan University student, had just celebrated his twenty-second birthday and was on his way home when he was chased by a gang of thugs who preyed on college students. To escape them, Lee jumped over a fence and landed on electric railroad cables, then fell twenty feet onto the rail tracks, where he was hit by a train.

Lee was not expected to live through the night. He had sustained an electrical shock of 25,000 volts, which caused him to burst into flames. He had fallen onto the tracks below where a train had sliced the flesh off one shoulder, but incredibly, had put out the flames with the rush of air from the wheels. Lee's body was so mangled, blistered, and blackened that five people who saw him in the hospital fainted.

Although the medical staff at the emergency room informed his parents that they should expect their son to die before morning, his mother begged them not to give up hope. She prayed for a miracle.

Lee was given more than 170 pints of blood, and his mother offered 20 percent of her total body skin for grafts so that he might live. Within sixteen months of the horrible accident, Lee was exercising fourteen hours a day at a rehabilitation center. Soon thereafter, he was playing soccer and anticipating his college finals, thereby providing a living testimonial to courage and positive thinking. In retrospect, Lee realized that there were many occasions when he could have given up and accepted life as an invalid. But then he would realize that he had faced what seemed an inevitable death only to be granted a gift from God of a healing miracle. It was in those moments of awareness that he would resolve that he was a young man with a wonderful life ahead of him, and he would continue to struggle until he had regained his health.

On a bitterly cold winter's day in 1995, the tugboat making its way across the freezing North Atlantic near the Canadian shoreline ran into a shoal that gashed its bottom. Within a few moments, the boat turned over and threw its four-man crew into the icy waters.

David Barnes later recalled that the swirling vortex caused by the sinking boat was so strong that the suction pulled him under the water and pulled off his boots. When he rose back to the surface, he discovered that his three friends were gone.

The icy water was bone-numbing, and Barnes desperately clung to a small flotation tank that had popped to the surface. He estimated that he was about two miles from shore, and even though he was already half-frozen, he began to paddle toward land.

Night had fallen by the time he reached some ice-covered rocks on the desolate shore. With what seemed to be his final gasps of life, he pulled himself out of the water.

Barnes was now on land, but the windy, ten-degree cold was turning his soaked clothing into ice. Although he was exhausted, he knew that somehow he must keep moving or he would freeze to death.

Barnes tried to stand up and walk, but his numb feet would not support him. For a time, it seemed easier to give up the struggle, but he kept his mind focused on his wife, Carolann, and their son, Dwayne. He prayed that God would allow him to survive to be with them once again.

As painful as it was, Barnes managed to stand erect and lean beside a large block of ice until his feet and ankles froze into a solid mass, thereby providing enough stability to enable him to walk. For seven hours he kept moving until he came upon a cabin that was used by quarry workers. Giving thanks to God, Barnes was able to get a fire started and begin to thaw out his frozen limbs.

Meanwhile, in the Barnes home, Carolann had been notified by Search and Rescue that David and his crew-mates had been killed when their tugboat had keeled over and thrown them into the freezing North Atlantic.

When Carolann protested that she knew David would somehow survive, she was told that the terrible cold of the ocean would kill anyone. A few hours later, in prayer, Carolann felt a strong mental connection with her husband, assuring her that he was alive.

The next morning, quarry workers found a nearly frozen man in their cabin and rushed David Barnes to a hospital. An astonished Dr. Fred Brushett said that it was a miracle that anyone could survive the conditions Barnes had endured. To add yet another miraculous outcome to the story of the man who literally became a human ice cube, Barnes's feet did not have to be amputated, and only his toes suffered nerve damage.

As we have seen throughout this book, there are many kinds of healing miracles. Some occur when even the most optimistic of individuals doubt that any kind of remedy could possibly alter what seems to be the inevitable outcome of a dire event. There are even cases where those declared clinically dead have been restored to life.

On the night of March 21, 1993, thirty-two-year-old Ward Krenz was snowmobiling with two friends when they were caught in a sudden snowstorm. Deciding to speed across Iowa's frozen Clear Lake to seek shelter, Krenz lost sight of his buddies in the blinding snow.

He was also unable to see the 200-yard hole in the ice that loomed before him.

In the desperate run across the frozen lake, Krenz had accelerated his snowmobile to top speed, so he traveled about fifty feet before he reached the edge of the hole, and the vehicle landed in the water and began to sink beneath him. He could see the headlight of the snowmobile disappearing into the depths of the lake.

Then, he was in total darkness, and the cold water numbed his muscles so he couldn't swim. He had a fleeting thought that he didn't want to die, but his entire body felt numb, incapable of fighting what seemed to be the inevitable. He felt a sense of peace come over him, and he surrendered to the icy water of the lake.

Krenz's friends had gone as quickly as possible to get help, and members of the local Clear Lake volunteer fire department had responded. Krenz had probably been in the water for about thirty minutes when the rescuers arrived at the site. After nearly forty-five minutes of probing the hole in the ice with searchlights, they spotted the top of Krenz's crash helmet bobbing in the water. The rescuers could see that he was floating in an upright position with his mouth, nose, and the rest of his face underwater. Later, it was determined that a pocket of air in his helmet had prevented him from sinking to the bottom of the lake.

By the time the rescuers pulled Krenz out of the lake, he had been in the frigid water for about seventy minutes and submerged for about sixty of those terrible minutes. He was rushed to St. Joseph Mercy Hospital, six miles away, where one of the emergency room physicians declared that his body temperature was 74 degrees. He was not breathing, had no heartbeat, and was declared clinically dead.

Although the doctors didn't think there was much of a chance of resuscitating Krenz, they hooked him up to a machine that was normally used during open-heart surgery to assume the functions of the heart and lungs. The apparatus took Krenz's blood, ran it through the machine, warmed it, then sent it back to his body. Miraculously, even though Ward Krenz had been clinically dead for ninety minutes, the process restored internal warmth to his body until his heart was able to resume working on its own.

Krenz remained unconscious for three days, remained in the hospital for thirteen days, and spent six weeks in a rehabilitation center before making a full recovery. Initial fears that he might suffer brain damage because he had been without oxygen underwater for an hour were thankfully unfounded. Doctors explained that because Krenz had experienced such a rapid drop in body temperature, his metabolism had been turned off. His brain had not required oxygen because the cold had shut it down. *The Guinness Book of World Records* lists the miracle of Ward Krenz as the longest time an adult has been submerged underwater and survived.

On May 20, 1999, a Swedish surgical trainee was skiing with two companions near Narvik, Norway, when she fell headfirst into a river and became wedged between rocks and thick ice. The skis of the twenty-nine-year-old woman protruded above the ice and prevented her from being washed downstream. Her companions, also surgical trainees at the local hospital, tried desperately to pull her out of the frozen river by pulling at the skis.

When it was apparent that their efforts were futile, they used a mobile phone to call the emergency medical dispatch center at the hospital in Narvik. For a terrible forty minutes, the two medical students watched their friend struggling under the ice. Then she stopped all movement.

Another forty minutes passed before the rescue team arrived from the hospital. They immediately tied a rope around the victim's skis to prevent her from washing downstream. They then began cutting a hole in the ice to free her from the icy water of the river.

By the time they had freed the young woman, she had been under the ice for about an hour and a half. Although the rescuers began CPR, it was apparent that the woman was clinically dead.

According to *FireRescue* magazine (April 2000), an air ambulance arrived about twenty minutes after the rescue team had pulled the woman from her icy tomb. During the one-hour flight to the University and Regional Hospital at Tromso, an anesthesiologist on board performed oral end tracheal intubation and ventilated the victim with 100 percent oxygen. By the time the air ambulance reached Tromso, the unfortunate surgical trainee had been technically dead for three hours.

Immediately upon arrival at the emergency room, the patient was taken to the operating room. At that time, her body temperature was 56.7 degrees, more than forty degrees below normal. The doctors found no circulation, and her pupils were widely dilated and unresponsive to light.

A team of cardiac surgeons, anesthesiologists, and specialized personnel and nurses trained in CPR worked on the patient. Her body was ventilated and put on a cardiopulmonary bypass to warm her blood before recycling it to her body. An hour after the patient was delivered to the staff at Tromos, she had regained a pulse.

The young woman's complete resuscitation took nine hours, and she was placed in intensive care for one month. Fortunately, according to Dr. Mads Gilbert, the surgical trainee was extremely fit. In addition, it was theorized that during the first forty minutes of her icy ordeal, she was breathing through an air pocket in the flowing water. This enabled her to take in some oxygen as her body was cooling down.

After a period of intensive rehabilitation, the woman regained the use of her extremities, and her mental faculties were unimpaired. Although the damage to her fingers forced her to abandon her training as a surgeon, by Christmas 1999, she managed to ski by taping the poles to her hands.

On January 21, 1996, Brenda, a mother of two, was at home in Grand Prairie, Texas, when she began to experience chest pains. She got into her fiancé Jim's truck, and they set out for the hospital, about fifteen minutes away.

They had not gone far when Brenda, complaining of dizziness, fell forward into the dashboard. Jim stopped his truck and reached for Brenda. Her eyes were open and dilated. He could feel no pulse, and she was not breathing. Brenda appeared to be dead. Desperately praying that his layman's analysis was not true, Jim continued toward the hospital.

When medical personnel brought Brenda's body into the emergency room, the attending physician, Dr. Chavda, concurred with Jim's tearful diagnosis. Brenda had no vital signs. She had gone into cardiac arrest and was clinically dead.

Because he was dedicated to the preservation of life, Dr. Chavda placed heart paddles on Brenda's chest in an attempt to shock her heart into starting. As he performed CPR, the physician was concerned that even if Brenda could be resuscitated, she would suffer brain damage. If a brain is deprived of oxygen for more than two to three minutes, the patient is likely to experience severe impairment—and Brenda had been clinically dead for far longer than three minutes before she was brought into the emergency room.

The doctor was about to give up all hope for Brenda when one of the nurses detected a tear coming from one of Brenda's eyes. The emergency room became electrified with hope. Brenda was fighting to come back to life.

After forty-eight minutes of intense efforts on the part of the medical team, Brenda's heart was once again beating. Although she remained unconscious for a week, when she awakened, she had no brain damage at all. In addition, she did not have any memories of her ordeal from the moment she slumped forward in Jim's truck until she returned to consciousness in the hospital a week later.

On July 8, 2002, fourteen-year-old Luis Alfredo Pinilla of Santiago, Chile, was accidentally strangled while playing a game with some friends. Although he was rushed to the Padre Hurtado Hospital in Santiago, Dr. Ernesto Behnke declared Luis dead upon arrival. Dr. Behnke, the hospital's director, said that Luis's heart had stopped and that he was unresponsive to cardiac massage, medication, or resuscitation procedures. In addition, the pH of the teenager's blood was 6.7, which is incompatible with life.

Luis's parents could not accept the tragic death of their young son. They gathered their family, friends, and neighbors to form a prayer circle, and began to pray for a miracle from the Virgin at Lourdes. They believed that the Virgin would spare Luis because he was an altar boy and because he wanted to become a priest.

Later that evening, staff members at the hospital heard strange sounds coming from the morgue. After investigating, they found Luis Alfredo Pinilla breathing and very much alive.

Completely baffled, Dr. Behnke told the Santiago media that there had been no mistake. Luis was clinically dead when he was placed in the mortuary.

The Pinilla family and their friends rejoiced that their miracle had been granted. Their fourteen-year-old son had awakened in a morgue after medical doctors had declared him dead.

*I*n 1985, thirty-one-year-old nurse Heather Duncan severely injured her back while trying to lift a heavy patient at the hospital in Aberdeen, Scotland where she was employed. The disks in her lower spine were severely damaged, and she was in constant pain. After she had undergone several operations, she was informed that she would be forever confined to a wheelchair.

Heather found it difficult to accept such a negative prescription for the remainder of her life. She had heard that there had been as many as 400 authenticated reports of healing miracles at the shrine near the small village of Medjugorje, where a group of children had seen Mother

Mary standing on a cloud in 1981. In October 1990, after she had been paralyzed from the waist down for five years, Heather decided to act upon her faith in God rather than in conventional medical diagnoses, and she set out on a pilgrimage to Medjugorje in Bosnia-Herzegovina.

As she attended a prayer service in a graveyard near the shrine, Father Peter Rookey, a Roman Catholic priest from Chicago, laid hands on her head, then ran them down her arms and legs. Father Rookey laid his hands on Heather a second time, and asked her if she believed that Jesus could heal her.

It was then that Heather had the visionary experience that would lead to her healing miracle. She saw Jesus, not as his image appeared on a crucifix, but as he might appear if he were standing there before her, ministering to her paralyzed legs.

Father Rookey asked again if she believed that Jesus could heal her. Heather answered in the affirmative, and a voice in the back of her head told her to stand up and walk. To the cheers and joyful applause of the other pilgrims who attended the prayer service, Heather walked around the graveyard.

When she returned home to Scotland, she surprised her husband, Brian, by walking unaided into their home and asking how he had been doing at work. Although he could scarcely believe his eyes, he simply replied that it was wonderful to see her walking again.

The former nurse is convinced that her recovery was a miracle. Her longtime physician Dr. Catherine Legg admitted that she had no medical explanation for the sudden healing of Heather's back. The parish office in Medjugorje, which documents all healings that occur at the shrine, also confirmed that Heather Duncan had been healed of a crippling back injury.

✠

Many individuals claimed to have been healed at their homes in the United States or in other countries by praying to the holy energy present at such shrines as Lourdes and Medjugorje. About the same time that Heather Duncan received her healing miracle by conducting a pilgrimage to Medjugorje, Rita Klaus remained at her home in the United States and prayed to the Virign Mary at Lourdes to be cured of multiple sclerosis. Her prayers were answered, and her healing was confirmed by the Lourdes Medical Bureau.

he doctor peered intently at his charts. He was the foremost heart specialist in New York City and was well known for his diagnostic ability. He wanted to be certain his conclusions were correct. When a doctor tells a patient he or she will die, he must be absolutely certain.

When the patient was shown into the doctor's private office, the heart specialist looked at the balding, pleasant-faced man in the dark suit and told him that he had bad news. "Mr. Landone," he said quietly. "Your heart is in very bad condition. You have no more than two or three weeks to live. I suggest you prepare your affairs."

That ominous consultation occurred in 1925 in New York City when Brown Landone was seventy-three years old. Yet, despite the warning from the physician, Landone healed himself and lived to be ninety-eight years old. He died on October 10, 1945, in Winter Park, Florida, after a lifetime of helping to heal people of every disease known to humankind.

When he was scarcely three years old, Landone fell into a piece of running machinery attached to his father's sawmill in the northwoods of Minnesota. Once he was past the crisis, the boy spent his days in a wheelchair. During his treatment at numerous hospitals, Landone astonished his doctors by writing out prescriptions in Latin for other patients. He was crippled until he reached the age of seventeen, then he miraculously healed his crushed legs and taught himself to walk.

Later, he would tell others in his lectures and books that he simply awakened to the idea of a perfect set of legs. He thought constantly of the joys of walking and the healing powers of God. Gradually, he was able to move the injured limbs and, finally, they responded to walking.

Brown Landone completed his education with aid from tutors, and traveled abroad for several years. He graduated from a university with a degree in medicine and later became an ordained minister.

Dr. Landone claimed to have been summoned to London and selected for study in holy monasteries in the

Himalaya Mountains of Tibet. He said that he studied for two years at the Kagyudpa Monastery of the Red Hats and with the Yellow Hats at their monastery in Tungkhara. It was here that he became a practicing mystic.

In addition to his mystical healing powers, Dr. Landone made an economic survey of Germany in 1913 and became the Director General of the Institute of Arts and Sciences of Paris, France. He was also appointed by the president of France to act as a special envoy to the United States. Returning to the United States, he was editor-in-chief of the *History of Civilization* and acted as a consultant to the Ford Motor Company and the Metropolitan Insurance Company. He translated many foreign documents for Theodore Roosevelt and became known as a successful man.

When his fortune vanished in the stock market crash, Landone vowed to devote the remainder of his life to spiritual matters and to healing. At times, he saw more than 1,500 patients in a few months. Some of his more enthusiastic supporters claimed that Brown Landone was able to cure about 95 percent of the people who came to him for treatment.

Brown Landone was unusual in that he combined the practical approach to medicine with the spiritual elements of mysticism. He frequently prescribed regular medication instead of prayer. In his opinion, those seeking healing should never reject material aids, because everything belongs to God and is placed on Earth for a purpose.

According to Landone's manner of thinking, God is the essence, source, and substance of all things created by Him. Material means created by God are part of God's manifestation, and so was the exercise of spiritual powers.

Another of Landone's incredible healing abilities can be seen in the unusual success of his absent treatments by mail. His office files were filled with testimonials from people who had been healed through absent prayer.

Landone was fond of saying that he would never pray for someone, but only with them. He reminded his patients that Jesus had said, "If two agree on earth as touching anything they shall desire, it shall be done for them."

When he reached ninety-eight years of age, Dr. Brown Landone prepared for his funeral. Although he had the appearance of a trim, middle-aged man, he drew up plans for a memorial, wrote the sermon for his funeral service, and forecast the exact moment that he would die. A friend who was present at his side when Landone died said that after dictating several letters to friends, he lay back on a couch, closed his eyes, and passed on.

The unusual abilities of Brown Landone led many people of his day to believe in the healing effects of mysticism, and many books of America's practical mystic remain in print, including such works as *Greater Spiritual*

Responsiveness of Body, How to Turn Your Desires and Ideals into Realities, and *Do Four Things Now: Positism, the Great New Discovery of Power.*

 "Something good is going to happen to you," proclaims Oral Roberts.

"Expect a miracle!"

Undoubtedly one of the world's most enthusiastic leaders of healing services, Reverend Oral Roberts, the Pentecostal Holiness minister from Tulsa, Oklahoma, has appeared regularly on hundreds of radio and television shows. His more than 300 healing and evangelistic crusades have brought his gospel tent, his practice of the ancient healing ritual of "laying on of the hands," and the power of prayer to hundreds of thousands of suffering persons. To date, Roberts has written 120 books, including *Expect a Miracle, Miracle of Seed Faith, Miracle of Seed-Faith 2000*, and *Still Doing the Impossible*.

Oral Roberts was born in Pontotoc County, Oklahoma, on January 24, 1918, the son of Rev. and Mrs. Ellis M. Roberts. Many people who know Roberts today as a robust man in his eighties would be surprised to learn that Oral was a sickly, awkward child without the strength to pick cotton or help around his parents' farm. When visitors arrived, little Oral ran to hide because he stammered and stuttered.

When he was sixteen years old, Oral was playing in a basketball tournament in Atoka, Oklahoma. Just before the final whistle blew, the youth collapsed and lay writhing on the floor, blood spurting from his mouth. He was treated, then taken home and immediately placed in bed.

During the next six months, Oral's weight plunged downward from 160 pounds to a feeble 118 pounds. He was unable to use his legs until the Lindsay Saints, a touring group of evangelists from Lindsay, Oklahoma, prayed one night with the sick boy until dawn. Afterward, Oral said he felt the Lord's presence on his legs.

A short time later, Oral was taken to a gospel tent meeting in a nearby community. The physicians had diagnosed his lungs as containing a tubercular condition. Oral sat on a chair padded with pillows and listened to Brother George Moncey preach his sermon. When the healing part of the meeting arrived, Brother Moncey placed his hands on young Oral and ordered the illness to leave his lungs.

Suddenly, Roberts leaped from his chair. "I am healed! I am well," he shouted, dashing around the crowded tent. Not only were his lungs healed, according to Reverend Roberts, his stuttering condition had been completely cured.

On December 13, 1938, Oral and Evelyn Roberts were married and became the parents of four children. For the next several years, Oral Roberts preached and received his formal education at Oklahoma Baptist University and Phillips University. In 1946, Reverend Roberts was minister of the Pentecostal Holiness Church in Toccoa, Georgia, and held revivals throughout the southeastern states.

One afternoon, Clyde Lawson, a deacon of the Toccoa church, dropped an automobile motor on his foot. Lawson was screaming and blood was gushing from his shoe when Roberts arrived at the scene of the accident. Roberts said he knelt and prayed for the injured man. Suddenly, Lawson stopped screaming, completely mystified as to why the pain had stopped.

He took off his shoe and found his foot was perfectly normal. Neither Lawson nor Roberts could deny that a miracle had been wrought.

Reverend Roberts and his family returned to Oklahoma shortly after the incident and, after a time of restlessness, Roberts said that he received a call from God. Roberts was lying on the floor when he claimed to have heard the command: *"Get on your feet! Drive your car one block and turn right!"*

Roberts followed these directions.

Then, God said, *"From this moment you will heal the sick and cast out devils by My powers!"*

Reverend Roberts rented a downtown auditorium in Enid, Oklahoma, and held a large healing service. Numerous people were healed. One elderly lady had suffered from a stiff hand for almost forty years, and the condition was healed.

When people called Reverend Roberts a "faith healer," he replied that he conducted healing services. "Only God can heal," he has said repeatedly.

Roberts resigned his pastorate in Enid in 1947 and took over a series of healing services being conducted in Tulsa by Brother Steve Pringle. Roberts's sermons packed the gospel tent every night. It became his mission to develop an evangelistic ministry that would heal the whole individual.

Shortly after the services had been started in Tulsa, reports were circulated that a blind man had regained his sight. Hundreds of sick people came from towns throughout the Southwest, and Roberts was on his way as a famed leader of healing services.

One of the most widely traveled religious leaders in history, Oral Roberts and his healing crusades have journeyed to six continents. Reverend Roberts was perhaps the first minister to publicly launch the present interest in healing services conducted for large groups of people. The Oral Roberts Evangelistic Association is headquartered in the "Abundant Life" building in Tulsa, Oklahoma, where crusades are planned and launched.

Oral Roberts University was chartered in 1963, the same year that Roberts, who had always been proud of his Native American heritage, received the American Indian Exposition's award as "Indian of the Year." In 1965, ORU welcomed the first students to its campus, which has grown to include twenty-two major buildings valued at more than $250 million. The student body has swelled to nearly 6,000 students, who have the option of sixty-six undergraduate and sixteen graduate-level courses, from business education to theology. Oral's son Richard Roberts has served as president since 1993, and Reverend Roberts has assumed the position of chancellor.

For millions of people around the world who suffer from illness or disease, Oral Roberts's positive admonition to "expect a miracle" has given them the faith and the will to conquer despair and pain.

t 11:00 A.M. every Thursday morning for over forty years, hundreds of people have filled the Mount Washington United Methodist Church in Baltimore, Maryland, to receive spiritual healing. And at precisely 9:00 every night, those same people, along with thousands of others who suffer from physical, mental, and spiritual ailments, pause for five minutes to give and receive the healing energy that flows into them from God. This tradition, established in 1950 by Dr. Albert E. Day and the remarkable healers Ambrose and Olga Worrall, came to be known as the New Life Clinic.

Ambrose and Olga Worrall built an untarnished record as spiritual healers of astonishing ability. They worked privately to aid the sick and participated in countless miracles during that time. Children with twisted limbs, diseased organs, and hopeless prognoses came to the Worralls for assistance and relief. Adults from all walks of life sought their aid as well. A great number of these people improved as a result of the healing sessions, and many were cured.

The Worralls' method of spiritual healing was remarkably compatible with the pragmatic techniques used by most scientists. This was probably because Ambrose Worrall was an engineer and, as such, was a stranger neither to science nor to the scientific method.

Olga Worrall was just as scientific as her husband. She was not the sort of woman given to vague thinking and incoherent conversation. Indeed, five minutes spent talking with her was enough to convince anyone that she was a straight-from-the-shoulder person who believed explicitly in what she and her husband accomplished.

It was their willingness to provide direct, unequivocal answers to any and all questions that won the Worralls the respect of learned people everywhere. An interesting aspect of the Worralls' healing ministry was that they never took a penny in payment for their services.

After Ambrose's death in 1972, Olga carried on as best she could. She participated in a weekly healing service at the Mount Washington United Methodist Church and continued to offer both her prayers and her healing energies every evening to those people whose names appeared on her long list. Until her own passing in January 1985, Olga Worrall continued an unselfish devotion to her healing ministry.

We were privileged to know both Ambrose and Olga, and we had many opportunities to sit quietly with them and discuss the spiritual aspects of their work. Before Olga's death, we enjoyed a frank discussion concerning their ministry as healers. Here are some selected excerpts from our conversation:

Steigers: *How did the medical profession and the organized church initially respond to what you were doing?*

Olga Worrall: When we started in 1930, we had a rugged row to hoe. We were unconventional, and the church took a dim view of what we were doing. Somehow or other, theologians forgot that the very foundation of Christianity was built on the gifts of the Spirit, especially healing. Healing was practiced by the early church until a certain group of nonspiritual individuals decided that they were the only ones who knew how to interpret God to the laymen. The church and its people have suffered for this.

So all the odds were against us. The church was unsympathetic and the medical profession was rather suspicious. The more fundamental members were certain this was the work of the devil. When they tell me that,

I always say I stand in good company, because that is what they told our Lord when He healed. We plodded along in our own way. We never took a patient unless he was given proper medical attention or was under the care of a doctor.

Steigers: *What is it that a healer gives to one who seeks healing?*

Olga Worrall: Perhaps that extra ingredient that accelerates the normal healing of the physical body. We don't exactly know what spiritual healing is, but it may be akin to electricity. Of course, we don't know exactly what electricity is either. Perhaps someday science will discover the law governing spiritual healing, and then it will be used as an adjunct to medical practice and will enable people to get well much faster.

Steigers: *Has the attitude of the professional medical and clerical community changed toward spiritual healing?*

Olga Worrall: Yes. I would say after forty years of practicing spiritual healing the church now respects us. Healing results have been obtained, but we did not claim we were the ones who did it. Only God is able to heal, whether He is working through a medical doctor or a clergyman or a healing channel. Without God's power, you are utterly helpless.

Now, even doctors are more open to the idea of spiritual healing. I have met many, many doctors and they are, as a rule, very compassionate people. I find medical people are using spiritual healing and praying. The dedicated doctors know they are only channels for this healing energy. They use their skills to mend the body, then that something extra takes over and heals.

I feel the New Life Clinic has brought many ministers into contact with spiritual healing in a very simple way. Our healing services are ecumenical. Christians and non-Christians come together. God is no respecter of persons. We are all His children, and when we can have a coming together, then healing takes place.

We must teach our people how to prepare themselves for healing. We must learn to be still and hear the whisperings of God.

Steigers: *What do you mean by soul healing?*

Olga Worrall: I feel that people are soul sick when they don't have communion with God. Their souls cry out for this communion, and very often this soul sickness will reflect itself in the physical body. If you can bring peace into people's minds, assure them that they are God's children, that God is concerned about their well-being, that those dear ones who have passed on ahead are very much alive and are eagerly awaiting their coming, that we do live after death, then you can heal and bring peace to the soul.

Steigers: *Do you believe each human mind is part of the consciousness of God?*

Olga Worrall: Yes! You have a mind that functions outside of the body. There is something in you, something unexplained. You can call it the mind, the God-spark. It is in command at all times. You can describe the physical body; you cannot describe the mind.

Steigers: *How should the gift of spiritual healing be developed?*

Olga Worrall: I would suggest that every minister, doctor, and psychiatrist be taught to be aware of their gifts of the spirit and utilize these gifts fully and effectively.

Anyone who has a desire to go into medicine or nursing is often a natural-born spiritual healer. These people heal without realizing it. I have found very few doctors who are not healers, but many of them can't talk about it because the medical profession is so opposed to alternative healing. These dedicated doctors do use their gifts *sub rosa*, and many of them have told us that they pray before they operate. There are those, too, who are natural-born diagnosticians who receive this knowledge intuitively. They don't "study" intuition in medical school. I know many doctors who are truly holy men.

Steigers: *When you perform the laying on of hands, do you intuitively know what to do?*

Olga Worrall: Yes, I know where to put the hands. Certain states do not permit healers to put their hands below the shoulders as protection for unsuspecting people against unscrupulous, so-called healers, and I approve. However, if the healing is going to be performed in a doctor's office or under supervision, the healer can put his hands on any area of the body. I have found, though, that this really isn't always necessary; very often a hand clasp will heal the person.

When a person comes to me and says, "Help me," I find this need triggers off the spiritual healing at force within me. If I had my way, every church would have a development circle that would meet once a week under proper supervision to permit our young people to be able to experience spiritual healing. In the old days, families set aside a time for prayer where the parents and children sat around in a circle. Some families still maintain this practice, and there will always be young people who will develop healing abilities. God's healing work will continue.

✠

One of the individuals most admired by Olga and Ambrose Worrall was Harry Edwards (1893–1976), who was one of the leading faith healers in the British Isles and the president and cofounder of the National Federation of Spiritual Healers. Approximately 4,000 British faith healers manifest their healing powers through a wide variety of techniques. Some are simply bone manipulators who practice a form of chiropractic. Others are essentially hypnotists who rely on the power of suggestion to cure their patients. Still more are proponents of prayer who believe healing can best be produced through fervent devotion. Some are convinced of the curative power of the "laying on of the hands."

Harry Edwards was visited each year by as many as 10,000 people who flocked to his clinic after they had exhausted all other forms of medicine. Most of his patients were "first timers," people who had never before visited a faith healer.

Much of Edwards's work was devoted to absent healing. In one year, Edwards received more than 674,000 letters requesting some form of healing. "I know thousands of people who have been cured by Edwards," a British journalist told us. "He cured every imaginable illness or disease known to humankind."

Edwards also held mass healing demonstrations that were open to the public. Repeatedly, the ill and the lame were carried up to the stage to receive his ministrations, and many walked away from the arena without assistance. "Edwards probably cured more than 50,000 people," said the journalist.

Faith healing has always been a highly controversial subject for the medical profession, and as such, Harry Edwards became a very controversial person in the British Isles and was often the center of a swirling debate. The British Medical Association's official position on Edwards was that his cures were essentially used to treat illnesses that originated in the mind or nervous system. They yielded to treatment through suggestion.

But his patients argued that even if Edwards cured only those people with psychosomatic illnesses, he was still doing an incredible amount of good. Those who had thrown away crutches and received what they deemed to be miracle healings declared that it did not matter where or how the illness originated. The main object was to be cured.

In 1954, a member of the Archbishops' Commission on Divine Healing asked Harry Edwards to put in writing what he believed to be the power and procedure that lay behind spiritual healing. Among Edwards's written reply were the following concepts:

- Spiritual or divine healing comes from God.
- Healers are carrying out the commandment of Jesus to heal the sick.
- Healers themselves do not possess any healing powers. They are simply the human instruments of God.
- Spiritual healing occurs only within the framework of God's total laws created for human good.
- Angels may be appointed by God to assist human ministers in the process of spiritual healing.
- Healings do not occur as a result of God's personal intervention on behalf of a particular individual, overriding His established physical laws.
- Divine healing provides demonstrable proof of the human soul and the continuity of life.

*U*nfortunately, when many people hear someone referred to as a faith healer, they visualize an unscrupulous spellbinder with hypnotic powers, a lack of conscience, and a spiel primed for the collection plate. While one should always be cautious of any extraordinary promises made by an individual who claims to be a healer, an increasing number of reputable conventional clergy persons of many faiths are quietly becoming healers, as well as teachers and preachers. A wide-awakening of the clergy's mission to minister to their church members' physical bodies as well as their souls occurred in the mid-1960s and has continued to grow ever since.

In the mid-1960s, Dr. Charles A. Branden, a professor of religion and literature of religions at Northwestern University, conducted a survey on behalf of the National Council of Churches regarding faith healing among ordained Protestant clergypersons. More than 30 percent of the ministers who replied to his questionnaire reported that they had healed as many as sixty-four different diseases through prayer. Because the Branden Report was only a survey, there was no obligation for the ministers to submit detailed medical reports. Nevertheless, the respondents were very conservative in their claims.

Dr. Branden pointed out that in almost every case, the ministers declared that competent medical doctors had made diagnoses and that there had been medical treatment for a period of time. In one case, a cancer of the lungs had persisted for two years and had been properly diagnosed and treated by a physician. After the healing service, which consisted of laying on of hands, some ritual, and prayer, X-ray tests disclosed the condition had cleared. Six months prior to the report of the case, there had been no recurrence.

Another minister, from the Midwest, told of curing a thirty-seven-year-old woman of lung cancer. Only a week before the healing, she had been examined by several consulting physicians and told that she had only a few days to live. The minister prayed with the woman. She confessed her sins. She also forgave a woman whom she hated. Her lungs were clear of cancer on the following morning, and after several years, the woman remained cured of the dreadful affliction.

A Colorado pastor prayed with a Denver man who had been bedfast for almost two years. Physicians had unsuccessfully treated the patient's tubercular condition and, finally, had abandoned all hope of recovery for the man. Following prayer and laying on of the hands, a cure was immediately delivered and the man was back at work within two days.

Eighty percent of the healing ministers reported their cures were permanent. In many instances, several years had passed since the healing had occurred, and there was no evidence of a resurgence of the disease. Dr. Branden, like many others, considered any healing that lasted for two years to be "permanent."

Reverend Mervyn Rich, an Anglican vicar, was first introduced to the Christopher West International Healing Fellowship group in 1962, when doctors told Winifred, his wife, that she would just have to learn to live with a painful leg complaint. After a session or two with the healing group, the distressing condition was completely gone.

Reverend Rich became intrigued by the group and learned that they had derived their name from an eleven-year-old boy, Christopher West, who in 1960 was given a month to live by two London hospitals. The unfortunate lad had two cancers of the spine. One growth was removed through surgery, but the other was declared inoperable because the boy's spinal cord ran through it. His parents were given the grim advice that another operation would kill their son. After healing, the boy's twisted legs began to straighten, and Christopher West became a healthy schoolboy who ran and played with the best of his fellows.

Reverend Rich, approaching retirement, received the permission of the Bishop of Portsmouth to become the Christopher West group's official chaplain. At that time, Reverend Rich told a Portsmouth newspaper that the group conducted a type of healing performed by the early Christians.

"These people [the healers], who all feel they are doing God's work, are having to fight for the right to be accepted back into the Church," Reverend Rich said.

Upon his retirement, Reverend Rich opened a healing clinic in his own home. In addition to his healing work, the clergyman was still asked to conduct Orthodox Anglican services. Once, when asked to conduct Evensong at All Saints' Church, St. Helier, Jersey, he responded to the suggestion that he hold a healing session after the Orthodox service. He was surprised to see that most of the congregation remained seated and that their numbers were increasingly swelled by those who had waited for the Evensong to end.

On that same night, Reverend Rich led a woman to the altar who had been confined to a wheelchair for thirty years. Later, after responding to further treatment by the Christopher West group, the woman took the arm of the retired vicar and walked at his side down the entire length of the church aisle. Fifty patients received spontaneous and successful healing on this occasion.

✤

Apparently, there is absolutely no disease that cannot be healed by prayer. The ministers who have this gift of healing claim a lack of miraculous power in their hands. "There isn't any magic or strange power to it," declared an Episcopalian minister who regularly holds healing services. "It is not the minister's hands—but God—who does the healing!"

In 2002, another study yielding solid evidence that the power of prayer can heal was concluded by Professor Leonard Leibovici of the Rabin Medical Center in Israel. Professor Leibovici conducted a series of experiments with 4,000 patients over a six-year period. He determined that intercessory prayer had an effect on the outcome of a patient's illness, bringing about a shorter stay in the hospital and a shorter duration of the negative effects of the illness. According to Professor Leibovici's conclusions, prayer should be considered for use in clinical practice.

One of the most amazing examples of absent healing occurred with the participation of Agnes Sanford, the wife of an Episcopal rector from Westboro, Massachusetts. Mrs. Sanford, the daughter of a Presbyterian missionary to China, reveals the account in her inspirational book, *The Healing Light* (1947).

The patient was the eight-year-old daughter of an Asheville, North Carolina, doctor, who had been hospitalized with a viral inflammation of the brain and spinal cord. The child was paralyzed from the neck down, and a 106-degree temperature raged through her tiny body.

The young girl was also afflicted with continual convulsions, and despite prolonged sedation, doctors were unable to control the spasms. Death seemed only a few hours away until the hospital chaplain telephoned Mrs. Sanford.

Mrs. Sanford asked for one of Asheville's most respected physicians, who was also a personal friend, to place his hands on the child at precisely 9:30 P.M. "I'll begin my prayers at that moment," Mrs. Sanford said.

A witness to the incredible cure through prayer later said that the doctor entered the room, where a nurse was using chloroform to try to anesthetize the patient so that further convulsions might be prevented. At that time, convulsions occurred every three or four minutes. The doctor placed his hands on the child at precisely 9:30. He had no sooner touched the patient when a relaxed sigh rose from her lips, and she fell into a deep, natural sleep. The convulsions ceased and the child seemed very relaxed.

The following morning, the child was still sleeping peacefully. Her right side was no longer paralyzed and, by afternoon, life came back into her entire body. Ten days later, the patient was released from the hospital and returned to her home.

By the following Christmas, the child was completely cured and the grateful family enjoyed a blessed holiday. The girl grew into a vital, healthy young woman who was the joy of her parents.

Agnes Sanford herself had been healed from chronic depression when a Protestant minister laid his hands on her and prayed for her. Later, she declared that all people who pray should expect miracles. In her opinion, the Bible taught more than moral lessons. A spiritual energy called faith was revealed that was capable of healing all hurts, griefs, and failures.

Mrs. Sanford began her healing ministry in the 1940s, and she became a pioneer in the positive-thinking movement that maintained that God's healing work followed the laws of nature. In such works as *The Healing Gifts of the Spirit*, Mrs. Sanford expressed her belief that God could perform healing miracles through angels and good spirits. Together with her husband, and alone after his death, she taught groups about the power of prayer. She passed away in February 1982, after thirty-five years of a rich and rewarding ministry.

In 1997, the family of David Stewart, a retired Methodist minister, made a dramatic and unconventional decision regarding Mrs. Stewart's mother, who had been diagnosed with cancer and given six months to live. The minister recalled the biblical principle espoused in James 5:14–15 that those who are sick ". . . should call the elders of the church to pray over him and anoint him with oil in the name of the Lord. And the prayer offered in faith will make the sick person well." Then, when the Stewarts discovered that the oils mentioned in scripture were still available, they took the eighty-five-year-old woman completely off her medicines, began anointing her regularly with oil, and changed her healing regimen to natural supplements and herbal teas. She lived for four more years.

Stewart, who is a former university science professor as well as a retired Methodist minister, has authored *Healing Oils of the Bible* and has become an advocate of using the ancient oils in conjunction with prayer to accomplish healings in the twenty-first century. What Stewart came to realize, he explained to Fiona Soltes of the Louisville, Kentucky, *Courier-Journal* (December 12, 2003), was that the oils mentioned in scripture respond to prayer. "They have an intelligence not found in chemical drugs," he said. "They can only be created by God, not made in a laboratory."

Among the healing oils of the Bible employed by Stewart are the following:

Frankincense, which can be used for cancer, depression, allergies, headaches, and bronchitis.

Myrrh may be used as an antiseptic and to support the immune system.

Spikenard, although traditionally associated with perfumes and incense, may be used to treat allergies and nausea and may also be employed to elevate mood.

Hyssop is recommended for relieving anxiety, arthritis pain, and asthma.

The oils are to be directly applied to the body in small amounts, often combined with a "carrier" lotion or oil to dilute them. In addition to rubbing the oils on the body, they may also be smelled. According to Stewart, the sense of smell is directly connected to the central brain, rather than the frontal lobes. Because this is the part of the brain that processes nonverbal and emotional functions, the scent of the oils may accomplish emotional healing and somehow even increase spiritual awareness.

The biblical oils have become available through Christian bookstores, health-food stores, and private distributors. Annie Huskinson, a distributor for ABBA Anointing Oils, told feature writer Fiona Soltes that the use of anointing oils was "biblical" and "what the Lord says to do" when one is ill.

The National Center for Complementary and Alternative Medicine advises that such oils be carefully studied before being applied and recommends that those wishing to try them should discuss the treatments with their primary-care physician.

As strange as it may seem, an accident can bring about a miracle healing. In 1974, after surviving a terrible car crash near her mother's home in Manchester, England, thirty-two-year-old Sandra was told that she had suffered severe injuries to her spine. She was paralyzed and would never walk again.

Sandra's great passion had been ballroom dancing with her husband, Albert, and the couple had taken their kids to dancing classes four times a week. Accepting the doctor's decree that she was confined to a wheelchair for life, she settled into the day-to-day chores and challenges that came with trying her best to be a good mother to her children while she was handicapped.

Almost at once, Sandra began to experience sporadic pains and sensations in her legs. She told her doctors that she was able to wiggle her toes, but they patiently informed her that she was having an occasional muscle spasm. When she asked to be given braces and physical therapy, the doctors explained that she was undergoing denial of her condition. She must accept the reality of a life in a wheelchair. Sandra did accept that unhappy reality for twenty-two years.

Then, in 1996, while she was seated in her wheelchair in the back of their van, Sandra was thrown onto the floor when Albert suddenly braked to avoid hitting a car that had pulled out in front of them. Sandra's right leg received a painful blow, and she screamed out in pain.

Doctors at the hospital couldn't understand why a paralyzed woman was experiencing so much pain. Curious, they ordered an ultrasound examination of Sandra's spinal cord and discovered that the injuries had not been as severe as the physicians had believed in 1974.

After twenty-two years in a wheelchair, Sandra was prescribed physical therapy to help restore weakened muscles. Soon, she was able to stand up and slowly walk the length of her hallway. Sandra could now look forward to playtimes with her grandchildren and, perhaps, an occasional slow dance with Albert.

When Verne, who had been blind in his left eye for fifty-three years, walked into his optometrist's office in Grand Rapids, Michigan, the doctor exclaimed that he had just witnessed his first miracle.

Ten-year-old Verne had lost his sight in 1944 when one of his buddies accidentally hit him in the left eye with a clump of dirt. In January 1997, the sixty-three-year-old advertising salesman was walking through a mall with some friends when he walked right into a pole. Verne shook his head, a bit stunned by the accident, then astonished that he could see out of his left eye.

Verne's optometrist discovered that the blow had apparently jarred loose a cataract that had been clouding the lens of the eye. After fifty-three years of sightlessness in his left eye, Verne was now able to read with a pair of trifocal glasses. A regimen of exercises to improve his hand-eye coordination strengthened eye muscles that hadn't been used since he was ten.

Verne believed that divine intervention caused him to hit the pole on that day. He said that he had always believed in a divine being and that miracles do happen.

✛

Forty-four-year-old Lee awakened to his miracle of sight after a thug punched him in the head. One night in the winter of 1994, a brutish intruder burst into Lee's home in northern England, looking for someone who owed him money. When the hoodlum realized that he had the wrong house, he took out his anger on the blind father of four who tried to stand up to him despite his handicap.

After the invader fled the house, Lee began to feel dizzy and ill, and he went upstairs to the bedroom to lie down. He fell asleep and awoke about an hour later to the initial stages of a healing miracle. He was able to see patches of color.

Lee, a former truck driver, had been declared legally blind in 1990. His adjustment to being blind had been even more difficult due to the fact that Lee was unable to see his youngest son, who was born after the onset of his sightlessness.

By morning, Lee was able to distinguish shapes. By the end of the day, he was able to recognize his wife and three children—and to see his youngest son for the first time. The first thing that Lee did was to take his children to the park and play catch with them.

Lee's physician couldn't explain why Lee's sight had been returned by a thug's punch to the head. Both the doctor and Lee were satisfied to call it a miracle.

✤

The very fact that Ivan Schultz survived the brutal accident is in itself a miracle. In 1990, Schultz, then twenty-eight, was a pilot flying out of Vance Brand

Airport in Longmont, Colorado. He was working on an airplane engine when he bumped a piece of equipment, which caused the propeller suddenly to lurch forward and strike him on the head.

Schultz was thrown twenty feet by the blow. The left side of his skull was broken into four pieces—one large forehead section and three smaller ones that lodged in his brain. Remarkably, Schultz remained conscious throughout the horrible ordeal.

After a week in the hospital, he was sent home with his right side paralyzed and his skull stitched together with hundreds of tiny threads. The day before the accident, Schultz had considered accepting one of the offers that he had received from several major airlines. Now he was faced with years in rehabilitation learning how to walk, talk, and read again. He would never pilot another airplane.

As one of the therapeutic exercises designed to strengthen his right hand, Schultz was given a small ball of clay to squeeze. In time, the lumps of clay became recognizable objects. Excited by his newly exhibited creativity, Schultz's wife, Dena, encouraged him to take a class with Fritz White, one of the top Western artists in the nation and senior sculptor for Cowboy Artists of America. With White as his mentor, Schultz began sculpting tribal figures and symbols.

In 1995, five years after the terrible accident that had sliced away 40 percent of his skull, Schultz was named by *Art of the West* magazine as one of the top sculptors of Native American art in America. His piece, *Spirit Seeker*, received an honorable mention from the Plains Artists National Competition, and it was purchased for the city of Loveland, Colorado, in 1997. Today, Ivan Schultz's works are in great demand, and he is famous for his anatomically accurate depictions of Native Americans.

A good many readers of this book will have heard of Edgar Cayce, the famous "sleeping prophet" of Virginia Beach. When he was a young man working as a dry goods clerk, Cayce contracted a throat ailment and was told that he would never again be able to speak above a whisper. In 1901, a hypnotic practitioner helped Cayce fall into a trance, then stood by while he began to describe his medical condition in minute detail. By the time the trance had ended, Cayce had not only uttered a prescription for his inoperative throat muscles and nerves, he had accomplished a self-healing that left his voice fully restored.

Cayce obligingly went to "sleep" for thousands of other people for the next forty-five years. In each trance, he visualized the patient's body and prescribed remediation. In many instances his prescriptions involved drug products that had not yet been made available to the public, but were awaiting delivery in company warehouses. In other cases, Cayce prescribed herbs with rich natural sources of drugs for which orthodox doctors would one day write prescriptions for their synthetic counterparts. Cayce's much-chronicled talents may have been the result of intuitive knowledge, extrasensory perception, or the ability to draw upon some great universal psychic reservoir of wisdom. Whatever the source of his abilities, Cayce was able to give medical diagnoses, prescribe remedies, and give medical readings for men and women who were often not in his physical presence, so-called "absent healings." When Cayce died in 1945 at the age of sixty-seven, he had given nearly 9,000 medical readings while in a state of trance. Altogether, more than 14,000 Cayce readings on a variety of subjects have been recorded on 200,000 permanent file cards and cross-referenced into 10,000 major subjects.

In 1931, the Association for Research and Enlightenment (A.R.E.) was chartered in the state of Virginia as a nonprofit organization to conduct scientific and psychical research. In 1947, two years after Cayce's death, the Edgar Cayce Foundation was established. The foundation is the custodian of the original Cayce readings and memorabilia of the great contemporary seer's life and career. Both are headquartered in Virginia Beach, Virginia, and there are more than 1,500 A.R.E. study groups around the world.

"My father's unconscious mind was able to tap the unconscious minds of other people and draw information from them," Hugh Lynn Cayce once said to us. "He insisted that there is a river of thought forms and intelligence at another level of consciousness, and that this was the source of his information. This procedure apparently had nothing to do with mediumship as we understand it. He had no guides or anything like that. He had to do his own legwork, so to speak."

Hugh Lynn Cayce's son, Charles Thomas Cayce, became the president of the A.R.E. in 1976 after his father suffered a heart attack; Charles still serves the organization in that position. Hugh Lynn died on July 4, 1982, in Virginia Beach. Posthumously, a collection of his speeches concerning Edgar Cayce's teachings on Jesus and Christianity was published under the title *The Jesus I Knew.*

✦

A number of years ago, Brad Steiger and his colleague Loring G. Williams wished to test the possibility that ordinary people, under hypnosis, might be able to diagnose the health of people both physically near and far in a manner similar to that of Edgar Cayce.

Because the origin of many human afflictions is conceded to be psychosomatic in nature, it would seem that, as hypnosis deals directly with the subconscious mind, hypnotherapy might be an effective way to control many of our ailments. For many years, Loring G. Williams had excellent success relieving the symptoms of, and often eliminating the cause of, many physical disorders.

In his experience as a hypnotherapist, Williams had seen chronic and persistent allergies and severe skin conditions, such as psoriasis, completely disappear after hypnotic treatment. Many people came to him regularly with a wide assortment of aches and pains. Williams, however, always cautioned them that hypnotic treatment was *not* a substitute for medical aid. It could, in his opinion however, be a great supplement.

It was certainly nothing other than a desire to aid fellow humans in relieving their pain that inspired Williams to fashion the healing beam of a "mental flashlight." In numerous experiments, the hypnotist had instructed entranced subjects to "see" individuals in X-ray form and to diagnose their ailments and diseases. In these experiments, the subjects were told to see the illness, bone damage, or nervous condition as a "black spot." Once the hypnotized subjects had found the "black spots," they were instructed to "erase" the darkened areas with the beam of light from their mental flashlights. In all cases, these diagnoses would be passed along to orthodox medical doctors who could utilize the information as they chose.

Brad suggested that a friend of his, Reva S., might make a good subject for hypnosis. He knew that Reva and her twin sister had experimented with hypnosis and telepathy when they were girls. His assessment of his friend was correct; she proved to be an extraordinary subject at wielding the mental flashlight.

Each time she was entranced and told to seek out a subject's pain or disease, Reva would squint her closed eyes, furrow her forehead, and visibly apply great concentration upon the afflicted areas that remained unseen to our eyes. She would sigh, then say, "Okay. They're gone."

That first night when Reva became the healer with the mental flashlight, there were a number of witnesses present, most of whom were downright skeptical and unbelieving. Only a personal demonstration would satisfy them, and it seemed that all the dubious witnesses had a particular ache or pain for which they wanted to receive a treatment from Reva's mental "shining light."

Whether it was from power of suggestion or some kind of group healing process, headaches, sore muscles, and upset stomachs were dealt with quickly and effectively that night. Each recipient of Reva's light beam later testified that he or she actually felt a warmth suffusing his or her affected area.

A journalist friend of Brad's, who was extremely skeptical about the matter of healing through hypnotherapy, asked with a broad grin on his face if Reva might "burn away" a small cyst on his ankle. He had mentioned the lump to Brad before the session began that evening, and he explained that although the thing was adjudged benign by his family physician, it had appeared virtually overnight, and his doctor had recommended that it be removed by simple surgery.

But after the entranced Reva had directed her healing light upon his ankle, he declared that he actually felt the heat on his cyst. And when he lifted the leg of his trousers, the lump had disappeared.

In order to test the most unusual "mental flashlight" a bit further, Brad put in a call to his family doctor the next day and asked him if he would select at random a number of cases from his files and bring them to the Steiger home that afternoon. Brad explained briefly what they were attempting to achieve, and although the doctor was doubtful of any results they might attain by such means, he was not skeptical toward hypnosis. One of his instructors in medical school had accomplished a difficult leg amputation while the patient rested peacefully in a state of hypnoanesthesia.

Dr. B.J. generously devoted a portion of his day off in order to assist them with a number of experiments in out-of-body diagnosis. The modus operandi was quite simple.

Williams would place Reva in a trance and instruct her to travel mentally to a patient whose name and address was supplied by Dr. B. J. When she felt she had arrived in the presence of the target personality, Reva would describe the patient's physical appearance for verification by Dr. B. J. Once Dr. B. J. confirmed the patient's identity, Reva would "see" the patient in X-ray form and describe the particular ailments as she was able to perceive them in the hypnotic state.

Dr. B. J. was most favorably impressed by Reva's ability to accurately describe the target patients' physical appearance, but he expressed frustration with the vague and general manner in which she described the various ailments. Such terms as "abdominal area" can mean something quite different to a layperson than it does to a trained anatomist and physician. Although Dr. B. J. conceded that Reva did hit some of the ailments with a degree of accuracy, some of the other descriptions were obscured by her lack of knowledge of basic anatomy and her layperson's meager vocabulary of medical terms.

"But wouldn't this all be interesting if you hypnotized a trained medical student to do this sort of thing?" Dr. B. J. speculated.

Reva could apparently "see" blighted areas within the patients' bodies, but her ability to describe and diagnose them would be considered rudimentary to a highly trained diagnostician such as Dr. B. J. On the other side of the coin, Reva's inability to name the affected portions of the body would do nothing to negate her incredible ability to "shine the light" on these areas and implement their healing. Reva's unique gift can be seen in the miraculous case of Glenn's feet.

Glenn and his wife drove several miles to sit in on the experiments of Mr. Steiger and Mr. Williams solely as observers and witnesses. On the particular night they attended, a number of individuals had requested that Reva "shine her light" on them so that they might experience the results for themselves. Reva was going about the circle of witnesses "reading" their past and present health conditions. When she got to Glenn, she at once picked up on an old high school football injury and a more recent injury to his feet. After Reva had described the damage done to Glenn's feet, his wife suggested that Reva attempt to "erase" the great areas of darkness she perceived in that area.

Brad shook his head before Williams reinforced Reva's hypnotic suggestion. Brad had known Glenn for about a year and had become familiar with the painful history of his terribly damaged feet. Glenn had fallen out of a helicopter when he had been in the military service, and both feet had been terribly smashed. In three months, Glenn was scheduled to have all the toes and certain sections from both feet amputated. Physicians had tried every form of therapy and temporary repair throughout the course of ten years, and the last resort, amputation, was now all that remained for Glenn. He had already resigned himself to six months in a wheelchair and the awkward process of learning to walk all over again.

"Don't bother," Brad whispered to Williams. "There's no use. Glenn is scheduled for amputation in three months."

Williams merely shrugged. "Never too late," he said.

"It is in this case," Brad insisted. "The medics have said it has gone past the treatment stage. They've already set a date for the amputation."

"Then he has nothing to lose, has he?" Williams pointed out.

Brad could hardly argue with such logic, and he stepped back so that Williams might again direct Reva into shining her extraordinary mental light over the dark spots on Glenn's feet.

There is no need to prolong the story for the purpose of building suspense. A month later, an excited Glenn telephoned Brad to say that his scheduled amputation had been called off. Pleased, but puzzled, his doctors were talking in hushed tones about a "medical miracle," although they were at a loss to explain how the alleged miracle had come to pass. There were two more exciting developments in Glenn's case: 1) A medical journal arrived to take pictures of his feet for an article on the strange and sudden healing process that had taken place; 2) While walking with his wife during a vacation in

Chicago, his long insensate feet had developed blisters. He was rejoicing in the fact that he could once again actually feel his feet.

Brad Steiger and Loring G. Williams concluded from their series of experiments that diagnosis by entranced hypnotic subjects should only be used as an aid, as a complement, to orthodox medical practice. Healing is an art, as well as a science. One and one may always make two, but the same pill certainly does not work for every patient. There are so many variables and subtle mental factors involved in healing. The delicate relationship between doctor and patient, the patient's will to recover, and the doctor's own confidence in his ability to heal, all remain intangibles forever out of the reach of test tube and mortar and pestle.

In September 1993, Paul, a thirty-one-year-old construction worker from upstate New York, checked into a New Jersey hotel; he intended to visit the nearby amusement park the next day to fulfill his dream of bungee jumping. Paul went to sleep, but he was so hyped to bungee jump that his subconscious took over. Dreaming that he was at the amusement park jump site, he tied a bed sheet around his ankle, walked to the balcony of his seventeenth floor hotel room, and jumped over the railing.

Even if the bed sheet had been tied to something solid in the room, it wouldn't have mattered a great deal. Paul would have plunged to what should have been a certain death seventeen floors below.

Later, witnesses would describe Paul as a young man who definitely had a squad of guardian angels looking after him. Paul's plummeting body bounced off a lawn chair on a balcony four floors below his room, then bounced again off the hotel's canopy on the ground floor. He then landed on the roof of a convertible that was parked in front of the building with its motor running. The impact of Paul's body knocked the car into gear and it ran across the street and crashed into a bed store. Paul awoke beneath a pile of mattresses, wondering where he was.

Incredibly, Paul suffered only a few bumps and bruises as reminders of his real-life nightmare. The police filed no charges, but they strongly advised him to dream about something less adventurous than bungee jumping.

She was but one of many plaster images of the Immaculate Heart of Mary that had come from a mold designed by sculptor Amilcare Santini. Once the little statues had been dried in the sun, painted, and sprayed with varnish, they were attached to a panel of black opal. The panel measured 15 by 12 inches, and the image of the Madonna 11 by 8 inches. Thousands of these Madonnas were manufactured at a plant in Tuscany and sold throughout Italy and Sicily for three dollars each. Like many of the other similar statues, this particular Madonna was sold as a wedding present.

The plaque of the Immaculate Heart of Mary seemed to be an apt gift for Antonina and Angelo Iannuso, who were married in Syracuse, Sicily, on March 21, 1953. Although they were no longer regular churchgoers, the couple was pleased to accept the blessing of the Madonna and to hang the image on the wall behind their bed.

A few months after receiving the statue as a gift, Antonina and Angelo saw the first signs of a miracle. Antonina was pregnant and her body was wracked with agonizing pain due to toxemia. At times, the condition caused her vision to go dim and she experienced temporary blindness. Some days, the twenty-year-old bride found it difficult to perform even the easiest of household tasks. Antonina prayed devoutly to the Madonna for salvation from the pain and torment that afflicted her.

On the morning of August 29, 1953, Antonina was overcome by a painful seizure. Her abdomen twisted with pain and her eyes clouded. It was then that she glanced up at the little statue of the Madonna and saw tears streaming down her face. At first, Antonina thought she was experiencing hallucinations, and she shouted for her sister-in-law Grazie and her aunt Antonina Sgarlata to enter the bedroom.

Believing the young woman to be hysterical, Grazie and Aunt Antonina tried to calm her by yielding to her insistent demands that they look at the Madonna. They were astonished to see the image of Mary weeping profusely.

Later, they both testified that the tears were so plentiful they flowed down the face of the Madonna and into the hand holding the heart. It was the most incredible thing the two women had ever seen.

In a combination of fear and adoration, Grazie and Aunt Antonina carried the plaque outside and called to neighbors to come and verify the phenomenon. One by one, the awestruck neighbors confirmed the miracle of the weeping Madonna.

The unusual healing power of the weeping Madonna quickly manifested itself. From the moment that she had first glimpsed the tears, Antonina's painful seizures had begun to disappear. Her vision cleared quickly and her throbbing headaches became a thing of the past.

Antonina's husband, Angelo, was skeptical about the weeping statue until he witnessed a torrent of tears for himself. He noted that the tears flowed only from the eyes and from no other area of the statue. He felt the image and agreed that it was completely dry. It seemed unlikely that the Madonna's plaster body had absorbed moisture and was simply oozing liquid.

Mario Messina, a neighbor, removed the Madonna from the wall in an effort to discover some rational explanation for the miraculous occurrence. He found absolutely no moisture on the wall. Later, he unscrewed the image from its base and found that it was thoroughly dry on the inside. He wiped the statue and dried it thoroughly. Within a few seconds, two pearl-like tears glistened in the Madonna's eyes.

When the news of the weeping Madonna spread throughout Syracuse, crowds of the devout and the curious hurried to see the statue. With dozens of people attempting to push their way into the home and receive a healing blessing from the Madonna, police officers suggested that the Iannuso family hang the image outside. Once outside the home, the Madonna wept profusely and dozens of the crippled, the lame, and the ill gathered before the weeping statue, seeking to be brushed with a cloth wetted by the Madonna's tears.

After a few hours, the crowds had grown so large that the police took the plaque to the station in an effort to reduce the confusion that was beginning to build.

Further credence was given to the statue when the Syracuse police removed the Madonna to their headquarters for safety. As the squad car moved through the street, a patrolman carefully held the statue on his lap. Within minutes, his jacket was drenched with tears. After about forty minutes at the police station, the Madonna ceased weeping, and the officers returned the statue to the Iannuso home.

On August 30, at 2:00 in the morning, after the family had endured a sleepless night, Angelo placed the image outside the house on a cushion to satisfy those individuals who had remained in the street, hoping to obtain a glimpse of the miracle.

The following day, the image was nailed above the door of the Iannuso home and people began collecting its tears on bits of cloth. A middle-aged man immediately claimed the healing of a crippled arm. A three-year-old girl stricken with polio, whose leg was encased in a network of stainless steel braces, was able to move her limb after being brushed with a tear-stained cloth. An eighteen-year-old girl who had been struck dumb eleven years before began to speak after her lips touched a bit of cotton wet with the Madonna's tears.

On September 1, a commission called on Antonina and Angelo for the express purpose of obtaining a sample of the tears for chemical analysis. Skeptical officers caught several tears in a chemist's vial and carefully examined the plaque for any pores, cracks, or irregularities. The Madonna wept throughout the examination and for nearly an hour after the officers had gone. Then, at 11:40 in the morning, the little Madonna ceased weeping forever.

The chemical analysis of the tears was released on September 9 and signed by four doctors, who decreed that in "appearance and composition" the liquid secreted by the eyes of the statue were "analogous to human tears."

Exactly one month after the occurrence, the statue was carried through the streets of Syracuse at the head of a procession of 30,000 people. The Madonna was devoutly moved to a railroad shed and encased in a glass structure capped with a bronze cross.

On a radio broadcast in December, the archbishop of Palermo, Ernesto Cardinal Ruffini, expressed the church's decree that in light of the diligent chemical analysis of the tears, the reality of the Madonna of Syracuse could no longer be doubted. On October 17, 1954, Pope Pious XII acknowledged the authenticity of the event and the miracle healing that occurred in the home of Antonina Iannuso.

Thousands have flocked to the shrine of the little Madonna, including more than a hundred bishops and archbishops and several cardinals. The little house where the Madonna first wept her tears is now an oratory where Mass is frequently celebrated. The image itself is enshrined above the main altar of the Santuario Madonna Delle Lacrima. A reliquary contains a vial of the statue's tears and a number of saturated cloths. Within a few short years after the miracle healing of Antonina Iannuso, more than 290 extraordinary cures were recorded, including 105 that have been deemed miraculous.

*T*hose hearty families who pushed into the frontier wilderness during the early 1800s were almost totally dependent upon folk cures for their medical needs. "Granny medicine" was dispensed by wrinkled old crones, whose wisdom supposedly increased as they aged.

Folk medicine is still practiced today in many isolated mountain communities, primarily in the South. For more than two centuries, a common Granny prescription for an open sore was to apply the mold scraped from aged cheese. Today, penicillin originates with a particular type of mold. Burn cases and sunburn blisters were treated by applying wet tea leaves. Modern doctors prescribe a

tannic acid solution. The active ingredient in tea leaves is
tannic acid.

Herbs such as peppermint leaves were also believed
to be good for curing flu and its complications. Poultices
of red pepper and mustard were supposedly beneficial
in drawing various illnesses and poisons from the systems. Persons suffering from pneumonia were steamed
with hot towels, wrapped in heavy quilts, and given
steaming glasses of hot water. Whenever a cold congested
a patient's chest, Granny usually prescribed a steaming
brew of hot water, whiskey, and bitters.

A friend who grew up in West Virginia shared with
us his memories of "Granny" Grant, who served the
country folk of the Appalachian Mountain region during
the dark depression days of the 1930s.

A tall, muscular woman with a loose-jointed stride,
Granny Grant's thick hands frequently brushed back a
thatch of black hair flecked with gray. Those powerful
hands were her pride.

"The Lord works miracles through these palms of
mine," she claimed. "He's healed thousands of people. It
ain't my doing. I ain't nothing but the vessel. He's the one
that heals."

Granny Grant would wander into an isolated hill community and spend a few days moving from home to home.
Her entire security depended upon the hospitality and
neighborliness of the traditionally clannish mountaineers.

Yet, without a doubt, news of her miraculous powers preceded her arrival.

"A woman down in Hazard, Kentucky, cured my leg," claimed an old miner.

But when the crippled and infirm arrived in Hazard, they heard that Granny Grant had left for Williamson, West Virginia. She seemed driven by a strong impulse to move through the hills and share her gift of healing.

"Just stay put in one place and she'll get around to you," became a familiar expression as the hill folk gathered on porches or before fireplaces and talked of the miracle woman.

In 1937, Granny Grant's tall, black-garbed figure was a familiar sight in the hills and hollows around Paradise, Kentucky. Whistling cheerfully, the seemingly ageless woman with the ruddy cheeks carried her worldly belongings in a small cardboard suitcase. Material things such as money and property never interested Granny. She was too busy healing.

"Any sick people in these here parts?" she asked of a crossroads grocery store owner, a few miles south of Paradise.

"Only one I know of is Mrs. Meadows," replied the merchant, carefully chewing a mouthful of Mail Pouch tobacco. "She's got a terrible goiter on her neck. It just seems to sap all the strength the woman has. She's been down in bed with it for quite a spell."

An hour later, Granny Grant was in Mrs. Meadows's bedroom. The patient was strongly in need of healing. An enormous goiter ballooned outward from beneath her chin, and her face was a livid purple.

"My name is Granny Grant, and I've been healing folks for years with these two hands of mine." The tall traveler spread her fingers wide and held her hands before the patient's eyes. "See those fingers? The power of healing is in 'em. Do you believe I can heal you with the touch of my hand?"

The flabbergasted woman nodded weakly. "I–I guess so."

"Do you believe that people were put on this earth to enjoy life and live like kings and queens every livelong day of their blessed lives?"

"Maybe some can," Mrs. Meadows said. "But my life is filled with trouble and misery."

"Then these hands will cure you," Granny Grant shouted, twisting her hands in a twirling motion. "Now, I'm going to lay my hands on your goiter, and don't be surprised if you feel something hot and powerful shoot through your body. That's only the powers of my healing hands. I'm just the vessel, y'know, for a power greater than me."

Mrs. Meadows stiffened as the strong, warm hands pressed against the painful goiter. Whatever doubt the woman harbored disappeared with the first surge of healing power that swept through her body. The goiter seemed to shrink before those hands were lifted.

"I felt it," shouted Mrs. Meadows. "I felt it."

"Of course you did," said Granny Grant. "Now, I'll stay here through the night if you invite me and give you treatments."

"I'm sorry. I didn't think to ask you to stay." Mrs. Meadows was embarrassed. She shouted instructions to her oldest daughter, Thelma, to make a place at the table for Granny Grant and fix up the sofa for her to sleep on during the night.

Throughout that night and far into the next afternoon, Granny Grant's healing hands were laid on the shrinking goiter. Twenty-four hours after her arrival, the knowledge-able healer predicted the goiter would disappear after a brief interval. Mrs. Meadows left her bed and ate at the family table for the first time in several months. Her sparkling eyes glistened with the renewed vigor of life.

"I don't know how to thank you, Granny," said Paul Meadows, the patient's husband. "We ain't got much money, but you're welcome to anything we have."

"No pay, my friend," said Granny Grant cheerfully. "I never take nothing but my food and lodging for doing my healing. This is my mission in life. Now, can you tell me of another poor soul who needs help?"

Paul Meadows furrowed his brow. "There's the little Hensley boy. Lives over on the other fork. Family's worried about him 'cause he's always having fits. Poor child just curls up anywhere and starts kicking and yelling."

"Give me the directions to their home, and I'll be on my way," said Granny Grant, throwing her few belongings into the dusty, battered cardboard valise.

Granny Grant wandered throughout the backwoods of Kentucky, West Virginia, and Tennessee doing her good work. Hitchhiking or walking through the rain or sunshine, she brought the "laying on of the hands" to thousands of people, and, if legends are to be believed, she cured many of her patients.

The laying on of the hands goes back to biblical times, and some of Granny's patients said that it could be compared to a crackling spurt of electricity. Those who had been healed by her laying on of the hands swore that a powerful, lightning-like force surged through her hands and passed into their sickened bodies. Granny Grant insisted that she was nothing more than the channel for a higher power and walked on through the hill country in search of others to heal.

✛

Another so-called "Granny" healer came to our attention through a correspondent named Clara, who told of a woman everyone in her hometown in Missouri called "Ma Pickens."

Clara began her account by telling of Meg, a young mother-to-be, who became distraught when her doctor said that the baby was not properly placed in the womb.

"He tells me that I must go into the hospital," Meg sobbed to Ma Pickens. "We can't afford a hospital. And it's too far away from home besides."

"That would be such a pity to go to the hospital when Mrs. McCarty is such a good midwife," Mrs. Pickens said softly. It always grieved her so to see people in anguish and pain. She was an avowed enemy of suffering.

"When do you next see your doctor?" Ma asked the expectant mother.

"Tomorrow," Meg sighed. "I'm certain that he'll place me in the hospital then. And what," she asked, her voice almost a sob now, "will become of the baby? Maybe it is so wrongly placed inside me that it'll die."

"Well, now don't worry," Ma Pickens said. "We'll see if we can't give your doctor a bit of a surprise."

Ma placed her hands near Meg's stomach and moved her fingers in a twirling motion.

The next day, when the expectant mother called upon Ma Pickens, she was glowing with happiness. She did not have to enter the hospital after all. Everything was as it should be. Her doctor had told her that by "some extraordinary means" the baby had moved to its proper place.

Everyone in the hills and valleys of Missouri's Ozark region knew that Ma Pickens was that "extraordinary means," because the charming mother of three now-grown children had been accomplishing extraordinary healings since the 1920s, when folks fell into poverty during the Great Depression.

According to Clara, Ma Pickens's strange power of healing advanced to the stage where she could listen to the voice of a patient over the telephone, detect conditions or pains in the caller, and, in the majority of cases, deal with and dispose of the illness without ever having seen the patient.

Clara said that she did a paper on folk medicine when she attended college in the early 1960s, and she interviewed Ma Pickens at that time. Ma, whose given name was Mattie, told Clara that when she first discovered her gift of healing, she seriously thought that she was going out of her head. But after a time, she looked on it more logically, telling herself that if this strange power was meant for her, who was she to deny it?

Although Ma Pickens had tried for many years to conceal the fact that she was different from other people in her little Missouri village, in retrospect, she realized that many strange and wonderful things happened to her as early as age three.

When she was six, she lived next to a woman who used to swear that young Mattie was continually bathed in a circling blue light. After her marriage at nineteen in 1922, a total stranger asked Mattie when she planned to begin healing.

Confused and startled by such an unexpected query, Mattie visited her mother to tell her of the unusual confrontation. Mattie said that she knew the woman must have been some sort of crank, but she found her words so unsettling.

"Then let us put them to the test," her mother said. "I have had this lump on my hand for some time now. If you have the gift of healing, make it go away."

Mattie Pickens reached out with trembling fingers to touch the lump. Then she burst into tears under some nameless tension and a strange feeling of paranormal power. In the sudden paroxysm of tearful release, Mattie's fingers brushed her mother's head.

Now the lump, which had been on her mother's hand, appeared in the same size and shape on her head. Then Mattie knew she had a very strange power.

In the next few moments, she completely removed the traveling growth from her mother's physical body. She had passed her mother's impromptu test of healing ability. Both women were astonished that Mattie had unknowingly developed and harbored such a talent. For the rest of the afternoon, they discussed the implications of such a power. If Mattie used it wisely, such a gift could be marvelous.

Mattie's husband, Les, who had not been present to witness the mysterious transfer and healing of the growth, scoffed at her apparent power of healing as utter nonsense. Then one night, he came home from work with a blinding headache.

"If you consider yourself a healer," he challenged her, cure me of this terrible pain. I've suffered from these headaches long enough."

"I didn't even know what to do even to attempt healing," Mattie told Clara, "but somehow my hands moved over Les's forehead without any personal control on my part. From then on, my husband suffered no more such blinding headaches."

Mattie's next patient was a man who had hardly been able to move because of a leg condition. When she arrived at his home, he managed to struggle up from the sofa and painfully limped over to meet her.

She placed her hands on the leg that had been so long afflicted. She grasped the precise area of the leg that had caused so much pain. Within five minutes, he was able to bend his leg and walk downstairs, something he had not been able to do for three years.

"From then on," Mattie Pickens said, "I could not stop myself. I was soon seeing forty and fifty patients a week from as far as four and five counties away. And I still found time to raise two boys and one girl and see that they grew up to be decent folk."

Clara said that Ma Pickens always refused to accept a penny for her healings, a generosity that she continued until her death in 1984.

✚

Although she was not a "Granny woman" operating in a rural area, Chicago's Deon Frey was a woman who possessed great natural healing abilities and performed little miracles wherever she went. In August 1969, when Brad Steiger lived in Highland Park, Illinois, a cyst suddenly appeared on one of his friend's throats after a period of rather severe inflammation. Although the doctors said that it was nothing serious, they recommended minor surgery to remove the unsightly lump, which was about the size of a small egg and protruded from the woman's throat as if she had an Adam's apple.

A few days before Ann was to report to her doctor's office, Brad suggested that he, Deon, and another healer stop by her home in Wilmette. At this point, Brad knew that Ann was rather closed toward the whole concept of unconventional healing.

In spite of Ann's protests, Deon placed her in an upright chair in her studio, and the two healers began to work on her.

Ann squirmed uneasily. "This really can't help," she said. "I appreciate what you want to do for me, but the doctor will soon . . ."

Ann became quiet. Something was happening.

The healers had been placing their hands on Ann, praying. Now Deon stepped in front of her and began to make light, stroking motions on her throat. Deon raised her fingers above Ann's flesh, but continued the stroking movements as she moved her hands higher.

Amazingly, the lump began to move, following the beckoning fingers. The out-of-place growth kept traveling until it reached the tip of Ann's chin—then it vanished!

Ann felt her throat in complete bewilderment. "It . . . it's gone," she managed to say. "The lump is completely gone!"

The demonstration was most impressive. Healing is among the most beautiful acts of human sharing on our troubled planet. All sincere practitioners, from medical doctors to chiropractors, from nutritionists to neurosurgeons, from medicine men to faith healers, have their part to play in alleviating human suffering.

arion, a forty-one-year-old clothing designer from Canada, was driving home late at night in her Mercury Capri along a road that she had traveled many times. As she approached a train crossing, she saw neither lights nor any kind of barrier, but suddenly a train was right in front of her. She slammed on her brakes and skidded into the side of the train.

The impact of the crash knocked her unconscious, and her automobile was wedged under the train as it moved down the tracks at thirty miles per hour. The crew was completely oblivious to the accident and had no idea that there was a woman in a car lodged under their train.

After about seven miles, Marion's mangled Mercury broke free and came to rest on the tracks. The train checked in at a nearby depot, reversed direction, and headed back along the route it had just traveled—and thirty minutes later hit Marion's car again. This time, however, the crew realized that they had struck something on the track and called for help.

The first rescuers on the scene did not believe anyone in the car wreckage could have survived the double impact. To their astonishment, they found the driver unconscious, but alive. They used the Jaws of Life to free Marion from the twisted metal of the car, then they rushed her to a hospital.

Although she had suffered a broken leg, a broken arm, and a generous assortment of bumps and bruises, Marion had survived what would have seemed an impossible one-two punch from a train. A Royal Canadian Mounted Police investigator explained that in this case the miracle lay in the fact that the first impact from the train had twisted parts of the car around Marion's seat, thereby providing a cocoon of protective metal that had saved her life.

Henry Rucker, a wonderful healer from Chicago, was a man who reacted to human need with warmth and love. A tall, African-American man with a face that could be as stern as an Old Testament prophet's just before he flashed a broad smile and made a wry remark, he was alternately a dispenser of admonitions about health and gales of laughter.

One time, after listening to Henry deliver a talk to a standing-room-only audience, watching him move gracefully about the platform and observing the charisma of the man, we teased him that sometimes he seemed like a combination of Bill Cosby and Father Divine. Henry takes his mission in life very seriously, but he is able to see the humor in his own humanity and in his own struggles to achieve a spiritual balance.

Once, we heard several people give moving testimonials to Henry's remarkable abilities as a healer. Then someone asked Henry if he was able to perform such techniques upon himself. In that soft-voiced, deceptively deadpan delivery of his, Henry admitted that he could not. There were incredulous gasps of disbelief.

"Look, folks," Henry explained. "I love people and I feel for them, and I want to help. Thank God, some people I can help. The love energy flows through me. God does the healing. It's not old Henry doing the job. But somehow there is still a subjective element involved. I can't heal myself. When I've got a headache, I take aspirin."

As Henry Rucker healed with love and laughter, he also sought to bridge the gaps that currently exist between theology, science, and metaphysics.

"I am a black, but I am a Westerner in this life, and therefore I am an activist. I want to stay involved with life. I want to turn on and turn others on and be a light. I don't want to just *hold* the light, you see; I want to *be* it, become one with it," Henry once told us.

"My own personal satisfaction is in knowing that I am doing what *I* am supposed to be doing. My pleasure is in seeing the things manifest that I have been told about.

Prominence and popularity are not nearly as important as seeing myself doing things that I know God would have me do.

"Our concepts of religion or philosophy are but measuring sticks to guide us. No matter where we are born, God provides us with these measuring sticks. If we were born in the Eastern countries, our concept of God would be quite different from that of the people of the West. But all views of God are valid. All these different roads lead to one point. There are only outward differences, and they are only semantic. The differences among religions are only the differences of language and interpretation. All religions are saying the same thing: There is something *outside* and, at the same time, inside of you—and you are an extension of this force."

From the beginning of our friendship with Henry Rucker, we became intrigued by the way in which Henry and his coworkers employed certain African dialects in some of their healing work.

"The particular dialect we use is not important," Henry explained. "We use these dialects in our healing work to change the vibrations in a place. By intoning certain vibrations, I can change people's entire concepts. By chanting, I could change vibrations in this room so that a person wouldn't want to walk through the door. I don't do demonstrations like that just to show off or to prove a point, however."

Henry was not at all into idle demonstrations of psychic prowess to impress the gullible and the easily led. "I just want people who might be influenced by me to be able to see life with a different set of values. I want my fellow humans to know that they and God have been one since they have been. I'm only a talented vehicle for the healing work. The results of that healing belong entirely to God."

When Henry's parents used to take him to church as a child, he would squirm about in the pew with tears smarting his eyes. He wanted to be a part of the church, but he could not conceive of a God that would make him frail and weak, then punish him for his ignorance and his lack of strength. When he began to get "pictures" through his mental faculties, his fundamental religious background set up an internal warfare that raged within Henry's psyche for years.

"I used to get these pictures of things in my head, and I was not able to understand what was happening," Henry said. "When nobody was around, I would talk to God and ask Him what He wanted me to do. I knew He wanted me to do something, but I didn't know what it was. At that time, though, He wouldn't answer me. I used to shout at Him, 'I know you hear every word I say! Why won't you talk to me?'"

When Henry was in the Army, "way back in 1944," a little Filipino, who seemed as old as the hills, gave him a message from God. "At the time, the old guy frightened me," Henry said, "because the things he told me seemed so ominous. Nevertheless, I was fascinated by what he said and I kept the things he said in mind."

In the mid-1970s, Henry returned to the Philippines, and he became fast friends with Dr. Tony Agpaoa, one of the more famous of the controversial psychic surgeons. The so-called "psychic surgeons" of the Philippines were extremely religious practitioners who claimed to be able to remove tumors and diseased organs from patients with only their bare hands. After prayers of healing, the wound left on the patient's body by the crude invasive surgery would seal itself and disappear within a very short time—sometimes within minutes.

"I know that there have been a lot of negative things said about Dr. Tony," Henry remarked. "Tony realized years ago that many bad things will happen to many of us in this field. We are going to be called phony, and we are going to be called black magicians and persecuted."

Henry had always felt that he could heal people, but he had been reluctant to claim to be a channel for such a sharing of the love energy. Then, however, Tony consecrated Henry's hands.

"This is the thing that really brought my life into focus," Henry affirmed. "My life was gaining full meaning for the first time, yet it was also becoming so very confusing. I had always had a fear of death, but now I understood that life did not end with the grave. I had always thought a lot about God, and now I was beginning to get a different perspective about the Father."

Dr. C. Norman Shealy, current president of Holos University Graduate Seminary in Springfield, Missouri, is a neurosurgeon with extremely impressive credentials. He was the former director of the Pain Rehabilitation Center in La Crosse, a faculty member of both the University of Wisconsin and the University of Minnesota as associate clinical professor of neurosurgery, author or coauthor of over 100 papers for professional journals, and author or coauthor of several books on unconventional healing. On the basis of Rucker's psychic diagnostic work, Dr. Shealy invited Henry and eight of his friends to come to La Crosse in January 1973 to test their abilities.

Dr. Shealy explained that seventeen patients were brought to his office. The healers were not allowed to ask questions. The staff at the Pain Rehabilitation Center had previously taken samples of the patients' handwriting and their birth data, which were made available to the healers.

After each patient had left the room, Dr. Shealy would poll the nine healers. "When we put it all together on personality and emotional problems, they were 98 percent accurate," Dr. Shealy said. "This is a fantastic record. The psychic healers provided elaborate discussions of the patients' family relationships, their marital problems, and so forth. Furthermore, they were 80 percent accurate on physical diagnoses.

"The psychic sensitives (healers) clearly gave the correct causes for the patients," Dr. Shealy explained. "Each one was different. For instance, one was an accident victim, another was an attempted suicide, one was suffering from an infection, et cetera. The psychics got each one of them."

Over the next several months, Henry Rucker and his fellow healers from Chicago interacted with Dr. Shealy's Pain Rehabilitation Center and psychically focused on approximately 180 patients. When we asked Dr. Shealy to assess Henry's healing abilities, he replied:

"Henry Rucker's interaction with some of my patients is not always something that I would say could be judged healing. I look upon it largely as psychological counseling, and I consider Henry Rucker to be the greatest psychologist I have ever met. In his ability to assess emotional problems, he is superb. From a physical point of view, he is reasonably good. On the basis of determining the cause of pain from photographs, birth data, and so forth, Henry and his friends were getting about 75 percent accuracy, which is very good."

Dr. Shealy completed an extensive evaluation of Henry Rucker's healing ministry in 1973 and encouraged him to form the Science of Mind Church of Chicago. Henry continued to heal with love, warmth, and laughter until his death on July 13, 2003.

In February 1994, Police Lieutenant Moore of West Sacramento, California, pronounced twenty-five-year-old Ricardo the luckiest man alive. At about 6:00 P.M. on February 3, Ricardo walked across some railroad tracks on his way to a bus stop. With his Walkman radio playing at high volume in his ears, he didn't hear the freight train approaching on one track and the passenger train hurtling along on another.

Ricardo was struck first by the westbound passenger train. The impact tossed him into the air and into the path of the eastbound freight train. When Ricardo opened his eyes and looked up into the faces of two frightened-looking railroad employees, his first thought was that he must have been mugged. He started to get up, then one of the men told him to lie still, the paramedics were on the way.

For the first time, Ricardo noticed that he seemed to be covered with blood issuing from a head wound. When he asked the men what had happened to him, they told him that he had been hit by one train, then slammed by another.

After only a brief stay in the hospital, Ricardo stated his firm belief that the good Lord had certainly been looking out for him. Other than some stitches in the back of his head and a temporary back brace, Ricardo was unharmed. West Sacramento Police Sergeant Hensley declared the whole incident of a man being struck in rapid succession by two trains and surviving with minor injuries to be "mindboggling."

On the way home from their elementary school one day in April 1953, Juan Angel Collado and Ramonita and Isidra Belen said that they had seen the Holy Mother in the small spring under some mango trees. At first, nearly all the people of Rincon de Sabana Grande, Puerto Rico, had either scolded the children or laughed at them for having told such a foolish story. But Juan, Ramonita, and Isidra never changed their story. They never added more details to make it more incredible. They never retracted any aspects to make it more believable.

Soon people began to wonder if the children were telling the truth, and more and more men and women had begun to come to the spring and its tiny stream to see for themselves if Mary would appear to them. But only the three children had been able to see the Holy Mother and speak to her.

Dona Nora Freise had been a paraplegic for more than four decades. One evening, she sat before the spring in the wheelchair that had carried her help- less body for forty-seven years and wondered about the truth of what the three children had excitedly told all who would listen. Dona Nora knew that the three little ones stubbornly held fast to their account of having seen the Blessed Mother at the spring. Was she being foolish in hoping that Mother Mary had truly appeared at the spring and had blessed its water with healing energy?

Dona Nora Freise believed that many times throughout the history of the church, children had been given an ability to see angels and holy figures that adults were sometimes denied. In her heart, she believed that Juan, Ramonita, and Isidra had truly seen Mother Mary just as they said they had.

She dipped a bottle into the stream and took some of the spring water home with her to Mayaguez. She would drink the holy water—and she would be healed!

A few days later, to the utter amazement of her family and friends, the woman who had been a paraplegic for forty-seven years was able to stand. Within another day or two, she was able to walk and permanently abandon her wheelchair.

The miraculous healing of Dona Nora inspired dozens of others to fill their own bottles, jugs, and pitchers from the spring. Crowds of pilgrims began to pour into the area.

Then the three children revealed that the Blessed Mother had told them that she would perform a miracle at 11:00 A.M. on May 25—a month and two days after she had first appeared to them.

As word spread of the impending miracle, huge crowds began to make their way to the spring. Because there were no serviceable roads that led to the stream, people were forced to walk a considerable distance to the appointed area.

Hundreds arrived on May 24 and slept overnight on the ground. The sick, the crippled, and the lame—all hoping for their own personal miracle—spread their bed-rolls as near to the sacred site as possible.

By midmorning on May 25, it was scorching hot. A brilliant sun ruled supreme over a cloudless sky. At exactly 11:00, however, it began to rain.

While some of those pilgrims clustered at the spring that morning might have thought the sudden rain out of a sizzling, cloudless sky was miracle enough, Mother Mary had an even more impressive display of holy might in mind. The rain was multicolored, and the assembled multitude was soon bathed in drops of water of every hue in the rainbow.

One of the pilgrims who received a miracle healing that day was Paula Carrasco of Miami, Florida, who had suffered for many years from a chronic neck ailment. Paula had been fitted with a metallic orthopedic brace that began at her waist, covered her chest, and ended at her jaw. It was, she said, like wearing a metal cage.

Specialists had advised her that there was not a doctor in the world who could heal her, and her husband, Felix Carrasco, had taken her to Puerto Rico only for a change of scenery. Neither of them had heard a word about the three children and the Blessed Mother of Sabana Grande.

As destiny would have it, they arrived in San Juan just as all of Puerto Rico was talking about the excitement that was to take place at Sabana Grande in a few days. At the same time, of course, they heard about the miraculous healing of Dona Nora.

Felix and Paula resolved to travel to Sabana Grande so that Paula might present herself to the Holy Mother for healing. When they arrived on the evening of May 24, however, Paula was so depressed at the sight of the thousands of hopeful men and women that she fainted.

When she regained consciousness, she was taken to the local health center at Sabana Grande. The attending physician advised her to rest, and she slept for a few hours in the special chair that she had brought with her. Ever since the orthopedic surgeons had fitted her with the torturous brace, it had been impossible for her to sleep in a bed.

At 4:00 A.M., Paula rose and began to make her way to the elementary school. Although it was extremely difficult for her to walk, she was determined somehow to reach the stream. Four National Guard members took pity on her and carried her nearer to the overflow of the spring, now known as the Stream of the Virgin Mary.

Later, as the miracle rain descended, Paula said that she saw many wonderful images, such as the Sacred Heart of Jesus and many flowers that seemed to float in the air.

Then she saw a nun standing near her. "Come forward, child, take my hand," the sister told her.

Paula said later that somehow this nun just stood out in the crowd. She was surrounded by thousands of people, yet all she seemed to be able to focus on was this beautiful, smiling nun. Paula wanted so badly to take her hand as she had asked.

The nun suddenly opened her arms and turned in all directions.

Paula now understood that no one else in the vast crowd could see the nun. Paula realized that this was not a mortal nun, but rather the Blessed Mother.

At the very moment of her revelation, Paula felt an electrical jolt in her head. She had no explanation for the painful shock, but she now felt that it was no longer important whether or not she would be healed. The satisfaction of seeing the Blessed Mother was enough for her.

Paula saw Juan, Ramonita, and Isidra pointing at her. The crowd was so thick around the children that she could not hear what they were saying, but it seemed to her that they wished to approach her.

At last a man came and told Paula that the three children were passing the word forward that Mother Mary wished someone to remove her braces. Paula was already aware that she could move her neck, so she offered no resistance when two men removed the oppressive braces. She was able to hold her head high and freely turn it. She was able to walk without help from anyone.

As she turned to walk away from the stream, people all around her began to shout and cheer that she had been healed.

When Paula and Felix returned to Miami and went to the specialists who had predicted that she would have to spend her life in a painfully uncomfortable brace, the doctors could hardly believe that they were examining the same woman. On each May 25 for many years to come, Paula returned to Sabana Grande and the Stream of the Virgin Mary to give thanks.

The site of the little stream in Sabana Grande has become so popular that plans were recently announced to construct a statue of Mother Mary that would be taller than the Statue of Liberty in New York. The grand-scale statue will be part of a projected 500-acre Mystical City complex that will contain various chapels, a food court and observation deck, and a radio and television station.

*T*he Malagasy called her *Ninebe,* "the Great Mother."

It was an affectionate title, which Ingara Nakling earned in her more than three decades of missionary work in Madagascar. Whether she was looking after the parentless children at the mission orphanage, leading a hymn sing in a jungle clearing, or administering a pill from her first-aid kit, "Ninebe" was setting an example for her adopted people. It was often a difficult life, but one that had borne such long-range rewards as a recent visit to the United States by one of her godchildren (now a native pastor in Madagascar).

When we met Ingara Nakling in October 1966, she

was eighty-five years old. We were amazed at the facility with which her mind could relate anecdotes about events that had taken place during the first days of her arrival in Madagascar, when she was in her early thirties. She was a tall Scandinavian-American woman with snow-white hair and sparkling blue eyes.

As she recalled some of her early adjustments to life in Madagascar among the native people, Ingara told us that one of the most difficult tasks in preaching the gospel lay in finding the proper words. "There is no word in their language for 'love,'" she said. "Love is central to the Christian faith; it would certainly be impossible to tell of Jesus without telling of his great love for all humankind. It was therefore necessary to combine existing word concepts."

What missionaries do in those first few weeks with a native people determines greatly the future success they will have. Missionaries have been killed in areas where an overzealous cleric offended the indigenous culture by a rash or clumsy act. This had been the case in early Madagascar, where an angry queen had once martyred any Christian on whom she could lay her hands. A later queen made Christianity the state religion, but this ecclesiastical fact did not deter natives in a remote region from slaying a Roman Catholic priest, who made the mistake of ripping a charm from the neck of a tribal chieftain.

"You have to learn to know the people," Ingara said. "You must learn their thinking. Most of all, you must show love."

"Why did you come here?" natives would ask her when she first arrived. "Why did you come to Fort Dauphin from across the great waters?"

"I came because I love you," would always be her reply.

Once the missionary lady had helped her inquisitors understand the concept of "love," the bewildered Malagasy were left to puzzle over the woman who came from far away in the middle of the United States because she loved a people whom she had never seen before. Ingara Nakling was soon called "The Lady Who Loves People" and then, "The Great Mother."

Ingara said that she had not always been assured and self-reliant during her experiences in the field. There was the time, for instance, when she was confronted with her first case of demon possession.

It had been quite late at night when she was roused from her meditations by an urgent knocking on her door. It was a number of her carriers, one of whom was a Christian convert.

"Please come with us, Ninebe," begged the convert, who was entrusted with providing the missionary with transportation through the jungle.

When she followed the men outside, she was confronted by the peculiar spectacle of one of the native bearers crawling toward the porch on his hands and knees.

"He has been possessed by a devil," the man nearest her whispered hoarsely.

"Cast out the devil," whined the afflicted one, who had by now reached Ingara's knees. "Cast him out and I'll lick your feet."

"That won't be necessary!" Ingara told the man, involuntarily moving her feet several inches away from his slavering jaws. She was confused. She had heard all the theories about "demon possession" being only a primitive synonym for mental illness. She conceded that this was often the case, yet sincerely believed that "possession" was a very real thing apart from mental aberration. She also believed, however, that Jesus of Nazareth had given his followers the promise that they could cast out demons in his name.

"My stomach!" wailed the man as he doubled over with cramps. "A devil is in my stomach!"

Ingara hesitated. She was undecided. "I'll get you a bromide."

"Cast out the devil!" pleaded the man. "You must first cast out the devil before you can heal me!"

The Christian carrier stepped close to Ninebe and told her that certain members of the man's village, fearing that his association with the missionary would lead to his conversion, had held him down, pried open his mouth, and allowed the witch doctor to pour "devil medicine" down his throat.

"The witch doctor fears your power and does not want to lose this man to your God," the convert told her.

Ingara looked closely at the possessed man's face. There was something about his eyes—something so much different from the glaze caused by either mental imbalance or a gastrointestinal disturbance. She made her decision. She sent one of the men for the native evangelist and ordered the other men to carry the moaning carrier into the house. Then, while a number of the older girls who stayed with her began to sing hymns, the missionary lady began to prepare for the ordeal.

It was a violent session of intense prayers with both Ninebe and the native evangelist beseeching God to cast out the demon that tormented the contorted man who lay before them. During the exorcism, the man's body levitated several inches into the air. Ingara kept her hand on the man's head and increased the fervor of her prayers when his frame floated free of the bed.

At last the man was quiet, and after a time, his eyes flickered back into consciousness.

"Do you know me?" the missionary lady asked him.

"Who doesn't know you?" he grinned. "You're the Lady Who Loves People."

"Are you feeling better now?"

"Yes," he sighed. "You and Jesus have chased the devil out of my stomach."

"Witch doctors used to look at me with bullhead eyes," Ingara Nakling remembered with a chuckle. It had not taken Ninebe long to grow much bolder in dealing with those whom the witch doctors had possessed, and her stalwart spirit often led her into spiritual duels with tribal priests. Once she stormed into a hut where a witch doctor was bleeding an ox of its blood and a dying man of his property in a vain attempt to banish a fatal disease. When the determined missionary lady ordered the witch doctor from the hut, he shook a sacred rattle at her and growled, "Now she's spoiled it all!"

Ingara Nakling spent the remainder of her days in South Dakota in a house filled with the echoes and memories of Madagascar and the people who came to return her love and respectfully name her their "Great Mother."

On Easter Sunday 1994, Tom Molrooney gave his brother Des a joyride in a twenty-five-year-old two-seater Jet Provost, once used as a trainer by Britain's Royal Air Force. As they soared across the skies over Colchester, Essex, England, Tom decided to treat Des to some upside-down rolls. On the second roll, Des's ejector seat broke free from its moorings and sent him through the cockpit canopy.

Des's helmet prevented him from being knocked unconscious by the impact, but he knew that he was in big trouble. He remained in the ejector seat for a few seconds before the safety belt snapped and he was free-falling at

120 miles per hour toward the ground 3,000 feet below.

Somehow, Des had remained calm. He reached for the parachute ripcord and pulled it, but the chute had been damaged when he fell through the cockpit canopy; he was now twirling around helplessly in the straps beneath the fluttering chute.

Des remembered holding his breath for the remaining seconds of the fall, never giving up hope that he would somehow survive.

He landed with a loud thud in a grassy area near a supermarket. Numerous onlookers ran to the scene, fully expecting to see an unlucky parachutist's broken and battered body.

Remarkably, Des was able to stand up unassisted and dust himself off. He had fallen 3,000 feet and suffered only minor bruising and whiplash.

✛

When experienced skydiver Klint Freemantle found that both his main chute and reserve chute had failed him while diving over Napier, New Zealand at 4,000 feet, he thought initially that his life was going to end on that summer's day in 1993. Ironically, his girlfriend, Tracey, had pleaded with him not to jump that day, and he had promised that he might make it his last. It now seemed that he would keep that promise in a most unsatisfactory way.

Then, far below him, he saw a small pond. He knew it was a one-in-a-billion chance, but Klint did not see any other options open to him. He undid his harness so he wouldn't drown beneath the parachutes if he survived the fall and aimed himself toward the water as if he were a guided missile.

Klint's father, Terry; sister Sarah; and Tracey, who had been watching him jump, ran in horror toward the pond, where they expected to find his body. Instead, a man covered in mud rose to greet them. Klint Freemantle had fallen 4,000 feet without a parachute and suffered only a cut over his left eye.

Some scholars believe that the Kahuna priests of the ancient psycho-religious system known as Huna practiced powerful healing techniques. The essence of Huna lies in the belief that we possess three souls: the *uhane*, a weak, animal-like spirit; the *unihipili*, a secretive spirit that sticks to, and often hides, another spirit; and the *Aumakua*, the older parental spirit, composed of both male and female elements, that has the low self (unihipili) and the middle self (uhane) under its guidance.

In psychological terms, one might say that centuries before Freud, the Kahunas of the Polynesian islands had discovered the conscious (uhane), the unconscious (unihipili), and the superconscious (Aumakua). Max Freedom Long, a schoolteacher who believed that he had cracked the Huna code in the 1950s, determined that Huna works as a system because it contains a form of consciousness that directs the "magical" healing processes, a force utilized by the consciousness. This force provides the necessary power and a visible or invisible substance through which the force can act.

The Aumakua, or High Self, is the "god" within each person. It is on this level above our waking, conscious level that we have the power to perform healing miracles. According to Huna belief, each individual's three spirits are surrounded, or encased, in three shadowy bodies composed of a substance called *aka*. Each of our bodies is fed by its own supply of *mana*, the vital force.

The low self (unihipili) utilizes simple mana; the middle self (uhane) feeds on a more highly charged mana-mana; the High Self (Aumakua) operates on mana-loa.

It is the role of the middle self to instruct the low self to store an extra supply of mana. This store of mana is to be held in readiness for the time when it is necessary to reach up the connecting aka cord and make contact with the High Self. It is the High Self, the "god" within, that brings about the desires expressed in the prayers of the three selves combined.

Max Freedom Long believed the central theme of Huna to be prayer and the obtaining of its answers.

In Hawaiian, the word for "worship" is *ho-ana*. Ho is from the root "to make." Ano is a seed. In the Huna code, we learn that the act of worship is the creation of a prayer "seed" to send with the accumulated mana along the aka cord to the High Self.

The Hawaiian word for the answer to a prayer is *ano-hou*. Once again, we find the root for "seed" and the root *hou*, which has several meanings. Hou may be translated to mean "to make new or to restore" or "to change a form or appearance."

Hou also means "to pant or to breathe heavily." Deeper breathing is necessary to accumulate the mana, which will carry the seed along the aka cord to the High Self. The mana helps make the High Self strong so it can answer prayers and make the seed idea grow into a reality.

Practitioners of Huna provide careful advice as to how best to send the proper pictures to the High Self: If you picture yourself in perfect health and impress that image on the low self as the "want" to be sent to your High Self, the low self will create and send a picture of you in perfect health. The way the High Self answers the prayer is to "make real" or "materialize" the picture into reality for you. This is the secret of secrets in Huna.

The picture of perfect health must not be one that includes your sickness. If you pray, "Heal my illness," the low self will make a picture of you sick and miserable and send it for the prayer. With it will go a picture of you wanting something and perhaps an image of you as well and healthy. The result is a muddle, and nothing is given to the High Self to change your condition.

You must believe that you are receiving perfect health. You must hold the thought of yourself as well and happy. If you do not, you inevitably send a sick picture to the High Self to spoil the good picture of perfect health that you have already sent up in prayer.

Making the picture of perfect health must be done with the use of the mana in order to get a lasting memory or thought-form picture to continue to recall and send frequently to the High Self.

Make and memorize your picture with breathing in order to collect the mana and give the picture enough strength to hold together while the High Self materializes it into actuality for you.

Instruct your low self to send the picture and plenty of mana to the High Self, like a telepathic message. The low self already knows how, so just set it to work.

Repeat your prayer action for healing at least once a day and continue until the answer is given. Have faith. Tell yourself that perfect health is already given on the level of the High Self and is already real. *Live* in the picture. *Feel* it. Keep your mind off your ills.

Long learned that some groups who studied Huna sought to project mana through the hands of the members of a healing circle, and to use their combined "wills" to make the mana flow into someone upon whom their hands had been laid. In addition, they might recite a prayer of healing, such as the following: "Father-Mother, we hold this friend of ours to the Light for healing. Give him/her life."

Long advised that one might compose a prayer that would suit all the members of a healing circle. Once the group has decided upon such a prayer, however, only the leader of the circle should recite it, while all other members remain with their hands on the subject in a quiet and prayerful attitude. The prayerful quiet should be held for at least half a minute, then the leader of the circle should end the group prayer with the words of the Kahunas of old: "Our prayer takes flight. Let the rain of blessings fall. Ah-mana-mana."

herry Hansen Steiger's belief that mind, body, and spirit are one first led her to study nursing. She then moved on to theology at the Lutheran School of Theology in Chicago, where she later joined the staff. A licensed massage-therapist, Sherry has conducted stress management programs for state boards of education, large business groups, the federal government, the U.S. Navy, and many religious gatherings. In the 1960s, she was the cocreator of the highly acclaimed Celebrate Life Program, and in 1972, she founded the Butterfly Center for Holistic Education.

In the latter years of the '70s, Sherry became involved with a group of prestigious doctors, many from the National

Institutes of Health. She became closely involved in the research, examination, and testing of such remarkable faith healers as Olga Worrall, holy men from India, and Native American tribal medicine people. After untold hours of discussing just what "holistic" medicine was to each of them—and focusing on exactly what the most important diagnostic and treatment modalities should be—it was unanimous that the process of "detoxification" was crucial. Fasting, sweats, and massage were all considered extremely important.

In 1978, Sherry was one of the founding members of the Holistic Healing Board through the National Institutes of Health and Education, Bethesda, Maryland.

It is Sherry's contention that the material for our creative transformation from disease to harmony, from illness to wellness, exists inside of us. Science has proven that an element cannot be changed unless its nucleus is changed. It is the same with human personality. The innermost self must change before healing or transformation can be accomplished.

As an important part of her personal program of self-discipline and growth, Sherry very often includes fasting as a vital means of cleansing mind, body, and spirit. It is her belief that there is a very important underlying truth surrounding the power of fasting in healing, since the practice seems to cross over all religions and cultures.

It is well known that the practice of fasting is an ancient one, which seems to have been employed by nearly every civilization. The Egyptians believed that one could preserve youthfulness if one fasted only three days each month. Hippocrates, considered to be the father of Western medicine, often prescribed fasting to treat critical diseases. Both Socrates and Plato are said to have fasted for ten-day periods to attain mental and physical efficiency.

The practice of fasting as a spiritual discipline can be found in virtually all religious traditions. From the Islamic point of view, Al Ghassali, a fourteenth-century poet and mystic, states: "Fasting stands alone as the only act of worship which is not seen by anyone except God. It is an inward act of worship performed through sheer endurance and fortitude . . ."

Paramahansa Yogananda, the great master teacher and healer from India, pointed out that when animals or primitive people are ill, they instinctively fast. He believed most diseases could be cured by fasting and said that the Yogis recommended regular short fasts (unless one had a weak heart).

Fasting is mentioned seventy-four times in the Bible. Moses fasted for forty days as he prayed and lamented over Israel's sin. Right after his fast, he was in direct communication with the Lord and was given the Ten Commandments. Elijah fasted for forty days, as did most of the prophets. Jesus fasted in the wilderness before his temptation, and he admonished his disciples that the body is the temple of the Spirit.

Just what is fasting? As a simple definition, fasting means to voluntarily abstain from food, except pure water, thereby giving rest to the entire body. When digestion and assimilation of food are suspended, the elimination of toxins is increased. Blood pressure decreases, and the process of healing is facilitated. Aging and sick cells are removed and regenerated, provided the disease has not reached an irreversible stage. Excess fat and abnormal deposits are consumed as food during the fast, while the cells and tissues of vital organs are preserved. The elimination of toxins or poisons from our systems seems to be the elemental process of the body, mind, and spirit.

In the body, toxins are harmful substances either produced as byproducts of bodily cell function, or from drugs and chemicals. They are eliminated from the body by the liver (in bile juice), by the kidney (in the urine), by the lungs (through exhalation of air), and the bowels (through elimination).

Often fruit juices are used to intensify the body's natural eliminative ability and to supply some nutrients. One can find many different types of fasts. There are fruit fasts, salad fasts, grape fasts, grapefruit fasts, apple fasts, millet fasts, etc., lasting anywhere from twenty-four hours to sixty days.

Here are some guidelines for fasting:

- Persons over forty or with chronic or acute disease or anemia should not fast for lengthy periods of time without supervision.
- The mind and emotions should be quiet while fasting.
- Don't fast while doing heavy manual labor.
- Sauna, steam baths, or sweats should be used in moderation.
- Drink *lots* of water—to wash out the system. Water permeates everything in our bodies and is the basic medium of our chemistry. Our bodies are composed mostly of water. It's easy to understand the wisdom of the ancients and the knowledge of modern medicine that focus on the cleansing of the body until it runs clean once again. After all, even to keep our cars running well, we are supposed to change the oil every 2,000 miles or so. And we live in our bodies.
- It is recommended that first-time fasters should limit their fast to three days. Any fasts longer than three days should not be undertaken until medical advice has been sought.
- One must be cautious when the fast is over and not break the fast with foods that are too heavy or by eating too much food. It is suggested to break

the fast with juices; then add fruit, then vegetables; then once again eat fresh fruit, followed by fresh vegetables; and slowly return to solids. There should be no grains, bread, eggs, or meat for a time equal to one-half the length of the fast.

rom the 1960s onward, through research, prayer, and inspiration borne of dreams, Sherry Hansen Steiger has initiated a number of innovative approaches to help people. One such program, a multimedia presentation that Sherry cocreated called "Celebrate Life," was performed all across the country at churches, schools, universities, and businesses. In addition to being an entertaining production, "Celebrate Life" also offered follow-up workshops, seminars, and retreats that lasted anywhere from several hours in length to a week, depending on the booking. Encouraging individual and group participation, the format involved the use of the media in and through various forms of music, dance, art, color, light, film, and slide presentations as a method for self-discovery and getting in touch with the spirit within. "Celebrate Life" proved to be extremely effective on many levels of body, mind, and spirit and proved to be a highly therapeutic means for revelation, expression, and healing. Because "Celebrate Life" was conducted in many cities throughout the nation, Sherry became well known as one skilled in several healing modalities.

In the early 1970s, Judy, an associate of Sherry's who lived in Colorado, became nearly hysterical when a police officer in Ohio called her to verify the identity of a badly beaten young woman who had been found lying in a driveway. From the items found in the victim's purse and the police officer's description of her size and weight, Judy was forced to conclude that the young woman who had been beaten beyond recognition with a blunt object and left to die was her beloved, beautiful daughter, Carol.

Defying the odds against her, Carol was revived in the ambulance as it sped her to the emergency room, where she barely managed to hang onto life. With broken ribs, bones, face, and head lacerations, she was in such critical condition that doctors did not expect her to last through the night. Judy talked to emergency personnel by phone, and the caring medical staff promised that Carol would be made as comfortable as possible in the hope that she would survive until Judy arrived. Judy made all the necessary emergency arrangements and boarded a plane from Colorado to Ohio.

When Judy arrived at the hospital, her daughter's injuries were far worse than she had anticipated. Carol had also lost so much weight since she had seen her last, that Judy could barely recognize her daughter. Fearing that perhaps Carol had been very ill and not told her, Judy was forced to face an additional cruel blow as the doctors told her it would truly take a miracle for Carol to survive—and *if* she did, there was no guarantee for the quality of life that she would endure. They promised to do the best they could to keep her alive, but without much improvement, Carol remained for some time in a coma-like state.

Judy contacted Sherry for prayer and help. Sherry was in Ohio at the time, but coincidentally was in the process of moving to Colorado. In the interim, the identity of the unknown assailant and the motive for the horrific attack on Judy's daughter would take on dimensions that evaded prosecution and conviction. Under the circumstances, Judy did what any loving mother would do—she focused her energies on saving the life of her daughter in preference to solving the crime.

Sparing no expense and refusing to accept the grim diagnosis and bleak outlook given to her by medical personnel, Judy took Carol to the best doctors and specialists and to the finest hospitals available as she sought a more positive and hopeful medical treatment. Repeatedly, she was told that there was nothing that could be done. Some of the most prestigious hospitals in the United States ran batteries of tests as they applied the best of cutting-edge science and medicine to Carol's injuries. But always, in the end, she was discharged with the same pronouncement: There was nothing further that could be medically done.

The final surgical procedure in an effort to aid Carol's recovery was so new that it hadn't been tried but a few times. Although Judy knew that there were great risks with this innovative and rare surgery, she could hardly have anticipated the outcome when a portion of Carol's brain disappeared into the blood/fluid suction machine. This terrible accident seemed to shut all doors to her daughter's recovery and the possibility of her again leading a normal life. As Judy's hopes were dashed, she was about to yield to the now-unanimous consensus that the only thing to do was to put Carol into an institution, where she would exist in a vegetative state and receive some care for whatever time she would have left.

But Judy couldn't bear to institutionalize her daughter. With a great deal of effort on her part, she finally convinced a nursing home not too far from her own home to take Carol.

Several months later, when Sherry was settled in Colorado, Judy invited her to visit on a weekend when

Carol would be with her for the day. Although there was no sign that her daughter had any recognition of her mother or of *anything* going on around her, Judy insisted on having this occasional time at home with her Carol. No matter what the official medical opinion might be, it was Judy's belief that a loving home environment might trigger Carol's memory in some sort of miraculous way.

When Sherry saw Carol in a quadriplegic state and bound up in a special wheelchair, her heart sank. Carol's limbs were stiff as boards and appeared to be not much more than bone with slight scar-bearing tissue covering them. Carol's arms were locked in a contorted position up and over her head. Without the ability to eat or to perform other bodily functions, she had colostomy bags hanging from the side of the wheelchair and feeding tubes inserted into her body. There was no conversation, no recognizable words, no glance or focus of the eyes, and very little sign of cognitive life whatsoever coming from Carol. To make matters worse, a low, guttural, agonizing moan, which gradually grew deafening and unnerving, would periodically issue forth from the unfortunate young woman.

Sherry did not know what she could do other than to pray with Judy, for this truly was far worse a situation than imagined. She knew it was beyond any optimistic or naive expectation to think that her nursing and theological background could invoke healing of any sort, other than to hope and pray that God would bring some kind of peace to Carol and Judy. The only thing Sherry felt she could do was to turn the bleak situation over—*completely*—into the hands of God and pray to offer some strength and encouragement.

It was during one of many later visits to Judy's home that something extraordinary caught Sherry's attention. Carol, Judy, and various other family and friends present in the living room had been enjoying music—sometimes just listening and occasionally singing along to tunes strummed on guitar. Without the intention to be cruel or inattentive, the members of the group had overlooked any unpleasant groans coming from Carol. They chose, instead, to focus on the positive aspects of the gathering and not make the situation any more stressful than it already was; the family and friends in Judy's home tried to fill the room with as much joy and love as possible. It was during these moments that Sherry happened to notice a most unusual expression on Carol's face.

Sherry saw what she deemed to be a look of recognition in Carol's eyes. Sherry carefully observed Carol, and after more verses had been sung, she had a notion that the music seemed to be reaching Carol's soul. It soon became clear to Sherry beyond the shadow of a doubt that there was something in Carol responding to the music.

When Sherry excitedly described the glimmer in Carol's eye and argued that the emotional aspects of certain songs seemed to evoke a response in Carol, the others in the group denied the possibility that such could be true. Sherry, however, was convinced this was an answer to prayer, and she asked Judy's permission to work with Carol in follow-up visits.

Since music seemed to ignite a spark in Carol's psyche, Sherry reasoned, perhaps through the use of music as therapy, more sparks of life could be renewed. She devised experiments using music, affirmations, tapes, poems, and songs all created just for Carol. Judy agreed to play them often, even when no one else was around.

Sherry noted that improvements were slow in coming for a while, but eventually there were changes that were noticed by all. Suddenly, it was as if something "woke up" in Carol's head. Judy said she thought she could even make out actual words that her daughter was trying to form. A whole new enthusiasm and ambition permeated the air. Although at first some doubted progress, there indeed were words . . . just a few here and there, but they gradually became more intelligible and deliberate.

What came next was amazing. Troubled by poor Carol's rigid and contorted body and with an invigorated feeling of the impossible becoming possible, Sherry began massaging the stiffness in Carol's arms.

In nurses' training, Sherry was far too sensitive to others' pain; she even backed off if the patient would react to a needle prick, so it was very uncharacteristic of her not to reduce her pressure when it appeared that Carol was in agony. In spite of Carol's loud groans that seemed to indicate great pain, Sherry continued massaging and using acupressure points on her arms.

Guided by some inner direction, Sherry spent untold hours over the course of time. She was relentless until she had achieved the goal of bringing one of Carol's arms all the way down to the armrest on her chair. Judy was in the kitchen at the time, pureeing some food for Carol, when Sherry let out a loud squeal of excitement.

As Judy rounded the corner of the living room from the kitchen, she barely caught a glimpse of what occurred. When Sherry turned to tell Judy what had happened, she let go of Carol's arm, and it immediately sprang back into its former contorted position. But Judy had seen the motion, and they were encouraged to continue with this painstaking effort.

During each subsequent visit, it took a lot of strength, persistence, and time to get Carol's arm to reach the armrest on the chair, but it didn't stay. The arm would always spring back after Sherry let go. Sherry eventually decided to have Judy *tie* Carol's wrist and elbow to the wheelchair armrest, first one arm, then the other.

Gradually, major improvements began to occur, even to the point where Carol exhibited controlled attempts to duplicate the relaxation of her arms while Sherry repeated autosuggestion relaxation exercises with her.

In time, it was hoped that Carol could do this herself and learn to let her muscles relax and unwind.

During many sessions, Carol would moan and carry on, but Sherry paid little attention and instead repeated to Carol how much she was loved. Sherry would remind Carol how beautiful and vital she was. She encouraged her to push through the pain and keep on with the various exercises in order to be healed. "*God can heal you, but you have to help*," became an often-repeated mantra.

Miraculously, one day Carol struggled with the suggestion of God's healing as she brought one of her arms down to the armrest from the old contorted position. There was a squeal from her that revealed her accomplishment and acknowledged both pain and excitement! A major breakthrough had occurred against all odds.

With more work and practice, Sherry thought that if Carol could bring her own arms down—even though it was still with great effort—there should be no reason why she and Judy couldn't work on helping her to control their movement in other directions. As the idea occurred to her, Sherry asked Judy for a lollipop to tie to Carol's hand, with the thought that this could be the first step in teaching Carol to feed herself. For a short time, Judy had been feeding Carol some baby food along with mashed potatoes and the like, which involved some struggle but was certainly a major step up from the tube feedings.

After many, many months of continued practice, at the nursing home as well as in Judy's residence, another astonishing thing happened. When one of the nurses was playing the tape-recorded relaxation and motivation tape for Carol, a loud "No" bellowed out from the patient! Carol continued to gain in strength to the point where Sherry asked Judy to fix a bowl of mashed potatoes and have a bunch of towels ready. It was time to help Carol feed herself. With much time and effort, a few setbacks, and many messes later, Carol enjoyed the occasional treat of trying new foods.

Although "No" was getting very old for others, it was still a miracle that Carol said anything at all. Soon she was able to say "Mom," which brought major tears to Judy's and Sherry's eyes, and the miracle progressed from there. It was as though Carol had been reborn, and step by step something new would be added to each day's blessings.

Sherry felt that it was time to call one of the well-known rehabilitation centers that had discharged Carol as having no further capacity or capability for improvement. When Judy did so and repeated the step-by-step process they had been through and the results of what Carol could now do, the doctors at the center denied that it was even possible. Dismissing all probability, they refused to take Carol as a patient, and it took another few calls to convince them to at least come and see for themselves.

After the specialists finally agreed to set a date and time to "take a look," they were flabbergasted at the healing miracle that Carol had undergone. The doctors told Judy and Sherry that it was beyond all scientific understanding as to how this could be. With a portion of Carol's brain missing—the part that governed speech and movement—such improvement was *impossible*. But they saw the proof with their own eyes.

Carol was admitted to the center. With a full-time rehabilitation regimen and a great deal of intensive therapies, years later Carol was in group therapy and carrying on fully intelligible conversations! She had regained complete use and control of her arms, and it was adjudged possible that some day she might even gain the ability to walk. Belief, love, massage, music, affirmation, and motivation may each have played a vital role in this miracle healing, but even greater was the power of God to reveal that miracles can and do occur . . . even against all odds!

*T*here is often great debate over the spiritual, moral, social, and medical decision regarding who, what, why, and how long a person should be kept alive in a vegetative state. With the technological capability of prolonging life indefinitely through life support, where does one draw the line? If there was a miracle in Carol's return from a "vegetative" state, couldn't there be hope for others who lie in their hospital beds under such a grim pronouncement?

Even in the early '60s, in her nurses' training programs and in various clinical and hospital experience, Sherry Hansen Steiger intuitively believed that on some level patients in comas could hear, feel, and understand what went on around them. At that time there was no medical evidence that comatose patients had this level of awareness, but in recent years that opinion has changed. Sophisticated technology and advanced scientific knowledge indicate that there is much more going on in the minds of the comatose than previously thought.

Many doctors argue, however, that certain facial motions and sounds—even muscle movements or twitches—can normally occur even with brain-damaged, vegetative, or comatose patients. Therefore, the question remains, how does one know if such sounds and movements are signs of real hope or if they only raise false hope for family and loved ones? Some doctors have expressed that keeping a patient alive or forcing treatment might even cause them more pain in the long run and that they should be allowed to die. Generally, most doctors concur that we still do not really know if a patient in a persistent vegetative state feels pain. For roughly the last thirty years, if the patient does not have a living will, the decision of prolonging the life of a comatose patient has essentially been left to the next of kin.

In response to the question, "Do patients in comas have awareness?" Dr. Jeffrey Frank, director of neurointensive care at the University of Chicago, stated his opinon (*The Chicago Tribune*, October 25, 2003) that at this point, all the doctors with our current level of medical technology can truly measure is the extent of the brain injury. Beyond defining the parameters of the injury, it is impossible to know if the patient is thinking. If the damage to the brain is major, the physicians can assume that any awareness that the patient might have would be limited.

Dr. James Bernat, neurologist and former chairman of the American Academy of Neurology's ethics committee, said that there is no laboratory test yet established that can truly ascertain the awareness of comatose or vegetative state patients. Currently a neurologist at Dartmouth College, Dr. Bernat said that the task of looking for evidence of clinical responsiveness and awareness of conscious life in a patient should be left to skilled medical examiners. Dr. Bernat was quick to add that on occasion the assessment regarding the level of awareness by even experienced medical personnel might be wrong.

That is what makes a miracle . . . miraculous. Once again, by definition, a miracle is an event that appears inexplicable to the laws of nature—as we understand them. At times when our sciences advance, we learn that our understanding of the laws of nature were limited. But by limiting either we may be putting restrictions on the unlimited supernatural power of God and on the miraculous, phenomenal power of love itself. The next story provides us with another demonstration of the profound power of both.

✦

It wasn't the fact that the first spoken words from her son in over nineteen years of complete silence were those asking for a particular choice of soft drink that startled Angilee Wallis—it was the miracle of miracles that Terry Wallis spoke at all! It was simply ironic that after nineteen years in a coma, Terry's first uttered words on June 12, 2003, were those requesting something so mundane and routine, as though no time had passed at all. And perhaps in his mind, it hadn't. This extraordinary span of missing time might in itself be considered a grace—to wake up after nineteen years of sleep as though it had been nothing more than a night's rest.

Time had *not* stood still for Terry's brother, mother, father, wife, and daughter. The whole family had maintained a nearly two-decade-long vigilance of faith and hope as they continued to visit Terry in the hospital, then eventually in the nursing and rehab center, never knowing if he was to ever wake up from this paralyzing perversion of life that had impacted all of their lives on one fateful evening.

On July 13, 1984, Terry Wallis and a friend were involved in a severe auto accident that had catapulted their car off the road and into the river below, ultimately coming to rest under the bridge. The crash was not discovered until the next day when the two young men's bodies were found. Tragically, the driver died on impact, and Terry's injuries were so severe that he was left a comatose quadriplegic.

In spite of what they had been told by doctors and medical personnel, Angilee and Jerry Wallis's undying love for their son never wavered. The trauma's impact was magnified by the fact that Terry and his bride, Sandi, had just had a baby girl, Amber, born only six weeks before the tragic accident occurred. As Terry lay in a comatose state, he may have had little or no awareness that he had left behind a daughter who grew up viewing her daddy only in a seemingly petrified state and a wife who could do no more than offer a one-way communication to a lifeless husband about the joy this little girl had brought to her life.

Eerily, almost exactly nineteen years later, as Angilee devotedly sat by her son's bedside in Stone County Nursing and Rehabilitation Center in Mountain View, Arkansas, she was shocked by the sound of Terry's voice saying, "Mom." One can only imagine the elation she experienced as her son suddenly and miraculously awakened from the coma . . . and asked her for a Pepsi!

From then on, Terry's improvement has been steady and sure. His vocabulary and awareness have gradually increased, and he was considered inexplicably "fully emerged" from the cocoon-like coma in which he existed for so long. According to *USA Today*, July 9, 2003, doctors will intensify therapies, as many as possible, to advance his healing. A speech therapist works with Terry three days a week, and nurses are encouraged to communicate constantly with him in sentences that help him to think and to give answers requiring more than a "yes" or "no." Dr. James Zini, Terry's physician, explained that Terry had never been expected to regain a full awareness or cognitive level to any degree. Terry's continued improvement will involve a great deal of effort from a team of doctors and therapists and will also require immense patience and persistence from him.

Although Terry doesn't seem to understand the vast amount of missing time since the accident, Dr. Zini made the observation that Terry is beginning to realize he's in a very different world now. His baby daughter is nineteen. Ronald Reagan is no longer president of the United States. A whole new technology has come into being, including cell phones, the Internet, and satellite dishes.

Terry's long-term memory, however, seems to be acute. Unaware that his grandmother had passed away, Terry asked to see her, even reciting her phone number, which the rest of the family had long since forgotten. Step by step, his healing miracle comes more clearly into focus.

*T*he 1987 Christmas season brought unexpected tidings of bad news to Jim and Cindy Brockhohn of Forest City, Iowa. As if it wasn't distressing enough to rush their young son to the hospital with pneumonia, they would soon learn of yet another serious health complication. The next to the youngest of four healthy, wonderful children—two boys and two girls—fifteen-month-old Jimmy was probably too young to comprehend the wonder of the preholiday excitement, to say nothing of how his life was about to be altered.

While in the hospital, the doctors had asked permission to run some more tests on Jimmy, and the results confirmed their suspicions that he had cystic fibrosis. The Brockhohns were stunned when the horrifying news was presented to them. Cindy recalled how terrified and helpless they felt as they sat by their son's bedside, day in and day out, as his tiny little body lay under an oxygen tent. He had various tubes and IVs taped to his little wrists, then anchored with little pieces of wood, with more tape anchoring them to the bedside. Although this seemed like torture to them, they knew that it was routinely done on infants and young children to make certain the tubes weren't pulled out. More tests were administered, then repeated. The "sweat test," which is the official diagnostic procedure for cystic fibrosis, conclusively backed up the doctors' previous devastating diagnosis.

Cystic fibrosis is usually fatal in early childhood, and the doctors prepared Cindy, Jim, and the rest of the family for the grim likelihood that, at best, little Jimmy would live only to his teens. Jim and Cindy refused to accept what they were being told. They were both in the chiropractic profession, and their wheels began to spin as their own medical knowledge and thoughts, as well as their heartstrings, tugged at them to search out more possibilities than those they had been given.

James Brockhohn is a D.C. (doctor of chiropractic), DACBSP (diplomat of the American Chiropractic Board of Sports Physicians), a member of the American Chiropractic Association, Iowa Chiropractic Society,

U.S. Olympic Sports Medicine Society, and the International Federation of Chiropractic Sports. His wife, Cindy, a certified chiropractic technologist and radiological technologist, assists Dr. Jim in his practice at the Forest City Chiropractic and Sports Clinic. All those who know Jim and Cindy are aware that their commitment to their family, community, and chiropractic practice have them on a schedule almost impossible to meet, so it would be no surprise they gave their all to finding a positive alternative to a very negative prognosis.

"In desperation and simply refusing to accept Jimmy's fate, I asked myself, 'what can I do for him using chiropractic,' and I immediately researched everything I could get my hands on about cystic fibrosis," Dr. Jim told Sherry Steiger. Jim learned that one of the things that occurs with cystic fibrosis is that many of the cells of the pancreas die, rendering it less and less effective until the organ finally gives out.

"I asked myself, what if the cells were not dead, but the nerve supply *to* the pancreas was merely *impinged*, thereby cutting it off and not allowing the pancreatic cells to function properly," Jim said. Continuing, he described to Sherry that the nerve root supplying the energy to the pancreas is located at the T-7 vertebrae, the middle of the back.

Although, as the father of the patient, it was next to impossible to be an objective doctor, Dr. Brockhohn examined Jimmy himself and discovered there was indeed a misalignment at that very location, and it was bad enough to sufficiently reduce the nerve energy to the pancreas.

"Our belief was that it very well could be the cause of little Jimmy's problems," Dr. Jim said. "It gave Cindy and me great hope, but first we had to get him through the pneumonia."

Once Jimmy was well enough to be released from the hospital, he was allowed to continue to recover at home. It was the advice of the doctors to have the tests repeated when Jimmy was completely over pneumonia and the fever was gone. Relieved when there was no trace of pneumonia, the Brockhohns took Jimmy back for tests. The results reconfirmed cystic fibrosis.

Convinced that the cystic fibrosis would be cleared up, Dr. Brockhohn applied his research and skills in treating little Jimmy at home, adjusting the T-7 vertebra until it was back in a normal position. Then Cindy and Jim requested another test be done on young Jimmy to see what the results would be now, once the energy/nerve balance to the pancreas had been stabilized. Since there had already been quite a few tests performed on Jimmy, the Brockhohns had to almost demand to have the additional testing carried out, but more tests were administered and, just as Dr. Brockhohn suspected, the results came back *negative*!

Flabbergasted, the traditional *allopathic* doctors—to distinguish them from *chiropractic* doctors—could not believe these test results could in any way be accurate. They suspected something went wrong in the testing and that such results had to be faulty. It was *impossible* for the cystic fibrosis to be gone instantaneously. "It simply doesn't happen," they told Jim; now *they* were the ones insisting there be further tests.

Dr. Jim felt the frustration of the moment. His joy of having the test results come back free of cystic fibrosis was slightly dashed by sensing the skepticism of the medical doctors that this could be true. With complete conviction that the new tests were accurate, Dr. Jim felt compelled to explain his position.

Not wishing to create ill will, the Brockhohns first expressed their sincere gratitude and appreciation for the excellent hospital care and attention of the physicians, nurses, and other personnel who attended to their son. Dr. Jim then proceeded to explain that the denial and panic he and Cindy felt over the unsettling news led him to research another way of approaching this disease.

Reiterating his discoveries of the chiropractic view of how a misalignment of little Jimmy's spine could have resulted in the illness, Dr. Jim confessed that he performed spinal adjustments on Jimmy at home. This explanation, however, did little or nothing to alter the medical doctors' opinions; in fact, they told Dr. Jim that even if the nerve supply is cut off to *any* organ, it would *not* hamper the organ from still performing its duties and functioning well. So, the demand for further testing. The following day, these test results came back *negative* as well!

"In actuality," Dr. Jim explained, "they were even *more* negative than the previous day." The adjustments had removed the blockage and allowed the nerve energy to begin to flow. "The pancreatic cells were beginning to return to normal function as the nerve flow was being restored to the pancreas," said Jim.

The doctors then asked if the Brockhohns would be willing to take Jimmy to the highly respected University of Iowa Hospital in order to continue with more testing to be as cautious and accurate as possible in their mutual concern for Jimmy's welfare. Spending over nine hours at the University Hospital was time well spent as the additional tests run there were conclusive. The doctor who was the head of the cystic fibrosis wing at the hospital confirmed that it was true; Jimmy's cystic fibrosis was gone. The tests were all negative; there was no trace of the disease.

Today, seventeen-year-old Jimmy Brockhohn continues to be active, healthy, and in demand as an actor. Sharing an interest in acting with his dad, *both* Jims have appeared in television and silver screen productions. Jimmy has already been acting for about nine years and has been in many productions thus far.

Dr. Jim and Cindy Brockhohn believe the miracle they experienced with their son Jimmy served to strengthen their belief and faith that they can help other families stay healthy and strong through their profession.

"My goal as a chiropractic physician has been strengthened more than ever to be a *family* chiropractor, treating the little ones as well. Treating children at a young age with chiropractic helps provide good health later in life," Dr. Brockhohn said. Proud to have played a part in his son's care, Dr. Jim hopes he can reach others with the miracles of healing. Currently, cystic fibrosis affects approximately 30,000 children and adults in the United States. If chiropractic can restore the health of even a few of them, it would be wonderful!

As his alter ego, Komar, the Hindu Fakir, our friend Vernon Craig of Wooster, Ohio, has discovered many secrets of pain control. He has lain on beds of sharpened nails for hours at a time, walked up a ladder with swords for steps, and walked barefoot across twenty-five feet of hot coals. At one time, he was listed in the *Guinness Book of World Records* for three pain-defying feats: the world's hottest fire-walk (1,494 degrees F); the longest time on a bed of nails (twenty-five hours and twenty minutes); and the most weight borne while on a bed of nails (just under a ton).

While few readers will be likely to be interested in

mastering such feats of pain control as lying on beds of nails or walking up a ladder of swords, many will be eager to learn how to control the misery of a headache, backache, arthritis, or any other affliction that might decrease their full enjoyment of life. The seventy-one-year-old Komar has taught pain-control methods to thousands of ordinary individuals, as well as those who suffered from mental retardation or mental illness.

According to Komar, the first step toward pain control is to learn to relax mind and body together. When you are able to do this, you will find peace of mind. You will become a healthier individual, and you will find your true position in the ever-moving stream of life.

Once you find that wonderful peace of mind within yourself, you will realize that both personal and external problems may be neutralized through the peace that abounds within.

Komar believes that those who suffer from pain must first understand that pain is the body's natural danger signal. "Everything about your pain is not bad," he said. "Pain is a danger signal—an alert. But there is no use in suffering needlessly, especially when the cause of the pain may present little actual danger to the overall health of the body. Sometimes the stresses of daily living, the many tensions one experiences on the job, or the fear of there being something seriously wrong with the body can magnify the pain signals out of all proportion to the actual reason for the transmissions. There are all too many instances where certain stresses and tensions can so work upon the imagination that pain can be created when there is no need for a danger signal of any kind."

Today's medical science has established the fact that anywhere from 60 to 90 percent of the pain that men and women suffer lies in their minds; it's caused by frustration, depression, worries, and emotional stresses.

"Mastery of self, once attained, will control pain," Komar explained. "Through self-mastery, a person will become better in every aspect of life. There are universal truths that yield the self-mastery necessary to control all pains and afflictions of the physical body."

By self-mastery, Komar means mastery over one's own lower nature and the negativity that can dwell there. "You must learn to accept and to strive for that *I* that is within you," he said, "and you will gain the proper kind of self-love within. It will swell out and show and reveal itself to the world. You will not have to run around and tell everybody, 'I love you; I love you,' because when you love yourself, it shows that you love the rest of the world as well.

"You must learn to believe in yourself because, if you do not, you cannot convince anyone in the world to believe in you," he continued. "When you start to believe that you can accomplish things—that you can be whatever you want to be—then you have begun to believe in yourself. As you believe in yourself, you will gain a beautiful outlook on life and become more a part of the world. Instead of being in the world, you will become a *part* of it. This is highly essential. The mind is the working tool of the ego. Work and strive toward this development."

As children, we are programmed to believe in various things in regard to our world. This often leads to what Komar calls "environmental retardation." We must make the first move and begin to change our world.

"If our world is not a happy one," he said, "we must change it. Each of us has the ability to create a wonderful world and to live in a wonderful world. You, and you alone, are the only one who can do that, because you are the only one who lives in your own individual world. No one else lives in your world—unless you invite them to live there with you. If those persons you admit into your world are very negative individuals, then they will have an influence on your world and make it an unhappy one."

Komar suggests that in a moment of honest reflection and examination, one asks, "What do I really think of myself?"

If your answer is, "Not much," then he advises that it is ". . . high time you set as your goal the systematic and continued development of self-esteem and the strengthening of your ego. You must have a positive attitude. You must learn to be positive within every molecule of your body."

Komar warns his students that negative thoughts can cause almost any kind of illness—ulcers, blindness, paralysis.

"If you will yourself into a negative situation, you can become very ill," he said. "Start now building your ego to produce positive thoughts. You must learn to have a positive attitude around you at all times. You must have little goals that you set and reach in order to keep building yourself. You must not be afraid to strive for goals for yourself that might seem impossible to you right now. A positive attitude will lead you to expect the most of yourself as an individual and as a human being."

Komar lists the following as his "prescription" for the self-mastery that can accomplish pain control:

1. *Ego*—the magic of believing in oneself.
2. *A positive attitude*—which is so much more than merely positive thinking.
3. *Relaxation*—which goes hand in hand with physical exercise. Without first tuning the body, it is difficult to tune the mind.
4. *Proper breathing*—the Yogic breathing techniques of complete breath and rhythmic breathing, which everyone can learn, and which, once accomplished, will put each individual well toward the goal of pain control.

5. *Concentration*—the ability to focus the mind and remove it from external tensions.
6. *Meditation*—a passive form of concentration. Most people never achieve this state. It is the sheer ecstasy of being in tune with the subconscious, the superconscious, the universe, or the god-self, whichever has the better meaning to the individual.

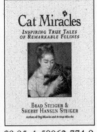